Early Childhood Education

Pembrokeshire College
Learning Centre
Haverfordwest, SA61 1SZ

☎01437 753267 ✉library@pembrokeshire.ac.uk
🖱 www.pembrokeshire.ac.uk/lrc

Return or renew online, or in person before the last date stamped below

-7 OCT 1997	25. JAN. ..9	30. MAY 2000	4/2/03
-7 NOV 1997		27. JUN 2000	2 6 ... 2007
5. JAN. 8	8.FEB. ..9	21/7/00	2 6 JUN 2007
28. JAN. 8	22 FEB. 9.9	22. NOV 2000	14 JAN 2008
25.FEB. 8	26. MAY ..9	-9. JAN 2002	27 JUN 2008
-8. APR. 8	25/6	7/11/02	-8 SEP 2008
	-1. FEB. 2000		
26. MAY. 8	28 FEB 2000	21/11/02	13 JAN 2008
16/10	25 MAR.2000	12/12/02	-3 MAR 2009
27 OCT. 8	27. APR 2000	8/1/03	25 MAR 2009
		6/2/03	28 APR 2009
-1 NOV 9. 8	22.MAY 2000	2/12/03	20 OCT
11.12.98		11/11/04	20 OCT 2009
-4 JAN ...9			

Early Childhood Education

Tina Bruce

Hodder & Stoughton

A MEMBER OF THE HODDER HEADLINE GROUP

A catalogue for this title is available from the British Library

ISBN 0 340 40735 2

First published 1987
Impression number 18   17   16   15   14   13
Year   1998 1997 1996

Typeset by BH Typesetters, Workington.
Printed in Great Britain for Hodder & Stoughton Educational, a division of Hodder Headline Plc, 338 Euston Road, London NW1 3BH by Redwood Books, Trowbridge, Wiltshire.

Contents

Dedication

To Sybil Levy

The gods did not reveal, from the beginning
All things to us; in the course of time,
Through seeking, men find that which is the better.
But as for certain truth, no man has known it,
Nor will he know it; neither of the gods,
Nor yet of all things of which I speak.
And even if by chance he were to utter
The final truth, he would himself not know it;
For all is but a woven web of guesses.

Xenophanes (c. 570–475 BC)

Acknowledgments

My thanks are due to Dr Marten Shipman, Dean of the School of Education, Roehampton Institute of Higher Education, London, who encouraged me to write the book.

Thanks also to Anne Findlay and to the Early Childhood team, with particular thanks to Lynne Bartholomew, Greg Condry, Joyce French and Shirley Maxwell, as well as Sylvia Young in the Early Childhood Archives, for their quiet but solid support.

I am grateful to Dan England for his care and trouble in taking the photographs; also to Patricia Juanette, Helen Tovey, Jill Vereycken and Mrs Ziranek, and the staff and parents of their schools, for the different kinds of help they have given.

Thanks to Chris Athey who helped me more than I can ever say to enjoy thinking about and working with young children.

Thanks to Una Bruce for feeding and caring for us while the book was finished; to Hannah and William Tom who bring meaning to Froebel's words, 'Let us live with our children'; to my parents Margery and Peter Rowland who still go to unreasonable lengths for their children, and who typed the manuscript. And special thanks to my husband Ian Bruce, who is the greatest enabler I have ever met, and without whose dedicated help the book would never have gone beyond its first draft.

Roehampton
January 1987   Tina Bruce

The author and publishers would also like to thank the following for permission to reproduce items in this book:
Open Books Publishing Ltd for the illustration on p. 70 taken from Goodnow, J. (1977) *Children's Drawing*; Heinemann Educational Books Inc, New Hampshire for the three illustrations on pp. 98, 99 and 100 taken from Ferreiro, E. and Teberosky, A. (1983) *Literacy Before Schooling*; Holmes McDougall Ltd for the diagram on p.60 taken from Roberts, M. and Tamburrini, J. (1981) *Child Development 0–5*; Rudolf Steiner Press for the illustrations on pp. 76, 77, 78 and 79 taken from Strauss, M. (1978) *Understanding Children's Drawings*.

Introduction

This book has been written for people involved in early childhood education, either at the stage of initial training or subsequently when practitioners wish to reassess and develop their contribution. It is not just for teachers, but also for nursery nurses and others with an interest in the field, such as health visitors, social workers and educational psychologists. I hope, too, that some parents will find it interesting and useful.

It attempts to re-assert, in a modern context, the principles of the early childhood tradition in education and to place them in the practical context of children's education today. This is not from a sentimental desire to continue in the path set by the early pioneers, but because there is a need to conserve in them what is of value and articulate it in more modern and acceptable language. Additionally, more recent theoretical and empirical evidence is introduced to produce a conceptual framework for today.

Work with children has been imbued with this tradition since the growth of formal education in the early nineteenth century. Such traditions are notoriously difficult to define and assess, but Lesley Webb (1974) forcefully makes the case for their reality.

> One must not overlook or underestimate the existence of the 'common law' of English nursery education, nor assume that because it is often unformulated and too rarely subjected to analysis, its writs no longer run (Webb, 1974, p. 4).

Although this statement refers to nursery schools, it is just as true for children under seven years of age.

Since the early childhood tradition directly explores how best to work with young children, it inevitably makes implicit assumptions about how the child is viewed — which might be as an empty vessel, as a person pre-programmed to unfold in certain ways, or a combination of both. However, these assumptions are likely to rest on a view of the child established in earlier times, when different versions of what a child might be were dominant.

The assumptions of the view of the child made by the early childhood tradition need to be re-examined, though not necessarily rejected (Bruce, 1985).

Part I of this book looks, in chapter 1, at different views of the child, in chapter 2, at three pioneer educators, and in chapter 3, at four 'giants'. It is a theoretical section to identify and support the ten educational principles of early childhood education and put them into a modern context. (Some practitioners may wish to take as read the establishment of the principles and omit chapter 2.) Part II covers the application of the principles through such topics as the curriculum, representation and language. It looks at practice in the light of recent research.

A synthesis of theory and practice is necessary because theory without practice is dead, while practice without theory has no direction. Theory *with* practice means that theory can inform practice enhanced by empirical evidence. It is then possible to see more clearly what to do and how. Working with children in this way is energising, fulfilling and challenging, as well as being highly skilled.

The book finishes with four action points comprising an agenda for change:

1   The need for a deeper knowledge of both child development and subject content.
2   The need to become less child-centred and more 'child-in-the-family/community' centred.
3   The need to work for better co-ordination and co-operation between existing services, resources and specialists.
4   The need for a sounder conceptual framework from which to operate, and better ways of assessing and evaluating it.

These points of action will guard against stagnation and enable the contribution of the early childhood tradition to be incorporated into a continually renewed and regenerated framework.

1 Three Different Views of the Child

People working with young children profess a superficial consensus in their approaches, but closer inspection reveals confusion and disagreement. This book explores whether there can be any pattern, any major areas of agreement, about how best to work with young children.

First, it is necessary to explore different ways of looking at the child. Until we are clear about the stance from which we view children, we cannot begin to work with them, nor is it easy to work together with other educators because our assumptions about the child are crucial in influencing our practice. One might, of course, ask if this exploration is really necessary. It would be easy to say that the only thing that matters in working with young children is a love of them, an enjoyment of them and a commitment to encouraging their maximum development. As far as this position goes it is true. It is amazing how far our gut reactions can take us and no one denies that some situations cannot be presented verbally. However, this does not allow the possibility of sharing our thoughts about young children's development with colleagues and parents. 'Gut reactions' are difficult to articulate, yet articulation is essential if communication is considered a high priority.

There are basically three main stances towards the child. One, the empiricist view, is that the child is an empty vessel to be filled (Scheffer, 1967). At the opposite end of the spectrum is the nativist view that children are pre-programmed to unfold in certain directions. These are combined in the third, or 'interactionist', view, which is that children are partly empty vessels, and partly pre-programmed, and that there is an interaction within and between the two.

Empiricism

The empiricist view implicitly subscribes to a deficit model of the child. The role of the adult is to identify missing experiences, skills, concepts and so on, to select appropriate experiences and transmit them to the child. This orientation came to the fore during the compensatory education movement of the late 1960s with Bereiter and Engelmann as clear proponents (Engelmann 1971). Children are seen as something to be moulded into shape and to be given experiences which are appropriate and necessary for them to take a place in society. Habit formation is valued, learning is broken down into meaningful sequences — for example, children are taught step by step to tie their shoelaces, hold their knives and forks correctly, sing songs which are part of their heritage, know their letters and so on. In the early childhood tradition, empiricism has always held a place.

Depending on whether we support the view of the child as passive recipient or as active explorer of experiences, the adult's role in working with that child will completely change.

In other words, there may be agreement that the child is shaped by the events, situations, objects, or people that he or she meets, but there is disagreement over the nature of the shaping.

Nativism

The nativist or biologically pre-programmed view suggests that humans are biologically pre-programmed with a propensity to unfold in certain ways. This idea stems originally from the thinking of Rousseau (1762). Bower describes the nativist view (1974, p. 2), 'that human knowledge and human skill were built into the structure of the organism'. Typical supporters of this stance would be Gesell, Erikson (a psychodynamic theorist) and, more recently, Chomsky. For Gesell (1954, p. 13), growth is seen as being 'laid down by intrinsic patterning prior to and independent of actual experience . . . environment predicts preliminary patterns; it determines the occasion, the intensity, and the correlation of many aspects of behaviour development, but it does not engender the basic progressions of behaviour development. These are determined by inherent maturational mechanisms.'

Sophie (aged one year) begins to walk when she is ready, not before, holding the armchairs and moving further and further from one to the other in the room. This is supported by Erikson (1963, p. 11), another educationist of the nativist tradition: 'if we only learn to let live, the plan for growth is all there.'

Chomsky reasserts this stance when he claims that we have an innate propensity for language. The environment dictates the kind of language learned.

Of the above two polarised views, empiricist and nativist, Robert Dearden (1968) suggests that the nativist stance is the dominant influence on the early childhood tradition. Certainly its influence is strong. In that tradition there remains a feeling that adults might interfere in a child's learning by intervening in the wrong way at an inappropriate moment. Some aspects of the child's world are seen as private and sacrosanct. Children must play, develop creatively, with imagination. Adults can offer help, but never insist on it. They need to be highly skilled in the way they approach children. The home corner is one such sacrosanct area, with walls around it so that children can be away from adults in a 'world of their own'. Inevitably, this leads to a major emphasis on relationships with adults and peers, based on respect for the child's unfolding development. These assertions stem from the nativist influence on the early childhood tradition.

Dearden (1968) places both Montessori and Froebel in this category, but this view is challenged in later chapters of this book.

Inadequacies of either empiricism or nativism

Howard Gardner (1982) points out the dangers of adherence to one overarching stance. This tends to narrow the approach to problems rather than opening up the exploration of them. In fact, the early childhood tradition is too complex for one to say that it sees the child from a dominantly empiricist or a nativist viewpoint.

Different emphases become the *Zeitgeist* of different historic periods. Certainly the nativist view of the child has had its periods of ascendency, especially in Europe, and empiricism has had periods of dominance, primarily in the USA. However, in reality the early childhood tradition is capable of embracing a much more complex approach than either of the two polarised orientations described. It can even be argued that, by polarising the different ways of regarding children, the early childhood tradition has been held back in its development. Either/or situations are rarely helpful in advancing thinking. It will be seen in chapters 2 and 3 that in reality the early childhood tradition has not taken extreme stances. As it develops it turns to the theories which seem to offer most support at each period.

Empiricism and nativism are two theories which ought to lead to entirely different ways of working with young children. In a sense, however, despite the great differences between them ideologically, they are often more polarised in theory than are their adherents in practice (Bruce, 1985). This may well be because of the inadequacy of the theoretical support that either of these theories alone can give the early childhood tradition. In the practical setting, people have to get on with the job in the absence of satisfactory theoretical support for their work. Both stances have, in fact, exerted strong influences over the early childhood tradition, but since in many respects they present diametrically-opposed ways of viewing the child, it is no wonder that there is a confusion and a lack of articulation about how the aims of that tradition can be reached. If early childhood education is to move forward, which it needs to do, more adequate ways of viewing the child are needed which are not embedded in obsolete or incomplete theories.

Interactionism

Recently the early childhood tradition has drawn support from a view of the child which is less polarised then either empiricism or nativism. This is the interactionist view which Tom Bower (1974, p. 241) summarises thus. He claims that development occurs as

> . . . environmental events interacting with maturationally generated behaviours. The major causal factors in cognitive development are behaviours interacting with other behaviours in their application to environmental events.

In other words, in this view of the child, which stems from the philosophy of Kant and later finds support in the philosophy of Popper, not only do the child's structures interact with and alter each other. There is interaction with what is external, but also there is interaction within the child. This is a much more sophisticated view of the child.

At the present time it also seems to be the most useful way of viewing the child. It implicitly reasserts the view of the pioneers of the early childhood tradition, that the role of the adult is critical. Adults are not seen as empiricist instructors giving out information and knowledge, rather they are seen as the means, the mechanism by which children can develop strategies, their *own* strategies, initiatives and responses, and construct their own rules which enable their development. Nor in this approach are children seen as nativist sole instigators of their knowledge, pre-programmed to act as they do, and held back, or helped as the case may be, by the variations in the environment. They are supported by adults who help them to make maximal use of the environment.

The key to the interactionist approach in early childhood education lies in the notion of reciprocity — that is, sometimes the child leads, sometimes the adult. For example, work by Gorden Wells (1983) has shown the importance of reciprocity in conversations between adults and children, so that adults do not dominate. This supports the view of the pioneer educationists.

In short, the interactionist view of the child supports the main principles of the early childhood tradition which will be considered in chapter 2.

The next chapter looks at the principles of the early childhood tradition and examines the work of three early pioneers of early childhood education, Froebel, Montessori and Steiner, through the interactionist view. Using this stance, it is possible to give their thoughts considerable support theoretically, although it is necessary to update the terminology which surrounds their work. Without doubt these thinkers have had great influence on the education of young children over the years, and the early childhood tradition has maintained a fairly steady course due to the work of an always small band of deeply committed workers continuing and developing the traditions. With increased attention now being given to the theoretical context against which to weigh the assertions of the early childhood tradition, it is time to move on and develop a modern synthesis incorporating the work of the early pioneers in early childhood education.

The aim is not to preserve an ossified, static approach to work with the under-sevens, but to conserve that which is

2 Ten Common Principles of the Pioneers — the bedrock of the early childhood tradition

The introduction stressed the pervasive influence of the 'common law' of the early childhood tradition and the need to understand and assess it if today's educators are to work effectively. This chapter looks at three of the most influential pioneers in early childhood education, and draws out commonalities between them which form the bedrock of that common law. They are *Friedrich Wilhelm Froebel* (1782–1852), *Maria Montessori* (1869–1952) and *Rudolf Steiner* (1861–1925). All have an international reputation and influence. Each has influenced schools in different parts of the world which purport to use their approaches; each has training colleges where teachers learn about their ideas; but, perhaps most importantly, all have significantly influenced mainstream education in Europe and North America. All three were skilled practitioners as well as being educational theorists. Each was concerned, amongst other things, with world citizenship, respect for persons' individual needs, poverty and the concept of community. Other pioneer educators such as Pattie Smith Hill (USA) (in Provenzo and Brett, 1983, p. 29), Margaret MacMillan (UK) and Susan Isaacs (UK) (1968), each working in the Froebelian tradition, have also been influential in contributing to these common principles and traditions, but not across all the criteria mentioned above.

The work of these pioneer educators with young children and their families reveals a set of common principles which have endured and still have a useful future. The agreements between them have been fundamental in creating the 'early childhood tradition'.

However, because these pioneers used very different descriptive language, often unacceptable today, and are the foci of superficially rival schools of thought, the common principles have become obscured. The commonality has been further obscured by the vastly different practical interpretation of the principles in the 'demonstration' schools of each pioneer. Ironically, it is in mainstream schools where the principles and practices of the three have come together, but this has been largely through osmosis and has often resulted in confused practice and ill-defined principles. If the agreements of the early pioneers were more clearly enunciated and understood, teachers would become more effective.

To summarise, the 10 common principles are as follows:

1   Childhood is seen as valid in itself, as a part of life and not simply as preparation for adulthood. Thus education is seen similarly as something of the present and not just preparation and training for later.

2   The whole child is considered to be important. Health, physical and mental, is emphasised, as well as the importance of feelings and thinking and spiritual aspects.

3   Learning is not compartmentalised, for everything links.

4   Intrinsic motivation, resulting in child-initiated, self-directed activity, is valued.

5   Self-discipline is emphasised.

6   There are specially receptive periods of learning at different stages of development.

7   What children can do (rather than what they cannot do) is the starting point in the child's education.

8   There is an inner life in the child which emerges especially under favourable conditions.

9   The people (both adults and children) with whom the child interacts are of central importance.

10 The child's education is seen as an interaction between the child and the environment, including, in particular, other people and knowledge itself.

Next, the 10 common principles are taken each in turn and supported through reference to the theories of Froebel, Montessori and Steiner.

1 Childhood is a part of life, not simply a preparation for it

Froebel, Montessori and Steiner agree that childhood is not merely a period when children are prepared and trained for adult life. It is a phase of life which is important in its own right although, as a by-product, the more richly childhood is experienced the more strongly the adult phase can be entered. The foundation stones are different in kind to the latter building material, but have an effect on the building as a whole.

Froebel saw the family as the most important first educator in the child's life. Joachim Liebschner (1985, p. 35) points out that Froebel believed women were not only important in their role as parents, but were capable of teaching children, too — a revolutionary idea at that time. The school was seen as a community, where home and school came together. Froebel (1887, p. 89) says: 'Let us live with our children, let them live with us, so shall we gain through them what all of us need.'

Children and adults learn from each other, and enrich each other's lives. Children are not seen as being in need of instruction on how to achieve an all-knowing adulthood. Childhood is seen as a different state from adulthood, one which takes from and gives to the community in its own way. Childhood is seen as a valid state in its own right, with the ability to contribute as well as receive.

Montessori also recognises the different nature of childhood. Again, she does not see the role of the adult as preparing children for adulthood. Childhood is a state to be protected and allowed to develop without damage in a specially prepared environment (Montessori, 1975, p. 13) 'that protects the child from the difficult and dangerous obstacles that threaten him/her in the adult world. The shelter in the storm, the oasis in the desert, the place of spiritual rest ought to be created in the world precisely to assure the healthy development of the child.' She argues that: 'The child is a personality separate from the adult.' Children need different treatment, but not, for Montessori, in a community where adults 'live with their children' in the Froebelian sense. Montessori argues instead for a separate environment where adults do not enter the child's world — except for the trained directress who liberates the child. Childhood is seen as a state with needs quite apart from adult life, existing in its own right.

For Steiner also there is no question of childhood simply preparing children for adulthood. Again, it exists as a period of life in its own right. In his philosophy, life after death is seen as another aspect of life before birth. There is therefore no question of childhood being 'preparation for life' but rather the idea of helping a newcomer to find his or her way. As children progress through the three phases of childhood, which involve, first, the 'will', then the 'heart' or feelings, and lastly the 'head', a fusion of spirit and body takes place. However, during the first seven years, the period of 'willing', the child's newly reincarnated soul must be protected. The environment is therefore carefully planned (Wilkinson, 1980, p. 6):

> While the adult can offer a certain resistance to his environment, the child accepts it, drinks it in. Thus the whole environment of the child should be a positive, harmonious one.

Steiner, like Montessori, separates the child from the world during the first seven years and places him/her in a carefully planned environment. They differ from Froebel who, while he also sees childhood as a stage with its own needs, distinct from adulthood, nevertheless sees the child as being in the community and the school as within that community. None of them sees childhood as simply preparation for adult life. Froebel, Montessori and Steiner all see childhood as a part of life, with its own particular needs and requirements, which are important in their own right.

2 The whole child is considered to be important. Health, physical and mental, is emphasised as well as the importance of thinking and spiritual aspects

Froebel, Montessori and Steiner all consider the development of the whole child to be of enormous importance.

Froebel saw the whole child as including the physical, spiritual, feeling and intellectual aspects of the person. Like Montessori and Steiner, he gave a great deal of thought to how the whole child could be developed through an appropriate curriculum. His notion of 'kindergarten', the garden of children, partly emphasises nature, partly community, and partly family.

Froebel addressed himself to the physical needs of the child through the 'forms of life', which involved the senses and first-hand experiences, to the feelings and imagination of the child through the 'forms of beauty', music, arts and crafts, nature, mathematics. He addressed himself to the thinking of the child through the 'forms of knowledge'. The spiritual pervades everything.

In his earlier work Froebel approached this through his 'Mother songs' (1878), 'gifts', 'occupations' and the garden (1887). Every experience presented to the child was presented first as a whole. The first gift was the soft sphere, the second gift was the cube, cylinder and wooden sphere. The third, fourth, fifth and sixth gifts cubes divided in different ways comprising small small bricks which would be built into a larger one. Only after being presented whole were they broken down into parts. The whole preceded the parts. Later, Froebel moved increasingly away from a set curriculum and became more interested in the process of play in the child, which he began to see as the mediator between two opposing forces, the natural and spiritual, emotion and intellect. In other words, he saw play as a means by which the child maintains the wholeness of his/her experiences. Play is a unifying mechanism and, for this reason, it is for Froebel the most spiritual activity of the child.

For Froebel, no single aspect in development is more important than any other. The whole child is the child where all aspects of development are enabled.

While Montessori believes equally strongly in the whole child, she approaches the concept quite differently. She postulates a simple-to-complex model. Each sense is developed separately and in isolation (visual, aural, baric learning and so on) through a sequence of carefully graded exercises.

She considers that, as children master each step and arrive at the end of a sequence, they are then in a position to use in a general way the skills acquired.

But, once the handicraft leading to the construction of vases has been learned (and this is part of the progress in the work learned from the

direct and graduated instruction of the teacher), anyone can modify it
according to the inspiration of his aesthetic tastes, and this is the artistic, individual part of the work (Montessori, 1912, p. 22).

Montessori takes each part of the child's development
and builds it to make the whole through her simple-to-
complex model (Bruce, 1984). This contrasts with Froebel,
who takes the whole and helps the child to find order in it
through an integrated approach in which play is the co-
ordinating mechanism. In their different ways, both Froebel
and Montessori stress the whole child.

Steiner is also concerned with the whole child. He
believed that we bring various qualities with us into life.
The whole person emerges as the four-fold picture of man
(Steiner, 1965, p. 21) involving the physical body, the life
body, the soul element and individuality.

Uneven development is seen as damaging:

It is always a matter of balance in human values. An all-round har-
monious development is the first aim, furtherance of special talent
can come later (Wilkinson, 1980, 16).

Steiner stresses different aspects of development at different
stages, all of which contribute to the whole adult, but are
important as phases in their own right. The wholeness
emanates from the way the spirit and body increasingly
fuse. First, the spirit fuses with the limbs (the period of the
'will' — 0 to seven years); then with the rhythmic system:
heart, chest, respiratory (the period of 'feeling' — seven to
14 years); then with the 'head' (the period of thinking —
from 14 years). Life after death is seen as another aspect of
life before birth. This all focuses on processes in the child.
Steiner is like both Froebel and Montessori in that he lays
great emphasis on processes in the child. For him, moral
sense, social feeling and religious attitude are influenced by
the experiences offered to the child. The wholeness of the
child's life is affected by nutrition (Steiner was a vegetarian)
and proper rest (rest and activity need to be balanced).

Steiner considers that the whole is reflected in each of
its parts. In this respect he is more like Froebel than
Montessori. The whole comes first. (This is unlike
Montessori's simple-to-complex model.) Nevertheless,
Froebel, Montessori and Steiner all emphasise the whole

child and whole environment of the child, which is considered in the next section.

3 Learning is not compartmentalised, for everything links

In the last section emphasis on the whole child was highlighted. In this section the wholeness of knowledge and the fact that everything connects is stressed. Nothing can be compartmentalised. Froebel (1887, p. 128) believed that:

> The school endeavours to render the scholar fully conscious of the nature and inner life of things and of himself and teach him to know the inner relations of things to one another, to the human being, scholar and living source and conscious unity of all things.

This 'conscious unity of all things' was central to Froebel's philosophy. He saw a unity between home and school, and community and nature, and between different areas of knowledge. We saw in the last section the links between different aspects of the child's development. Froebel (1887, p. 134) says:

> Never forget that the essential business of the school is not so much to teach, but to communicate the variety and multiplicity of all things as it is to give prominence to the everlasting unity that is in all things.

The soft ball (the first gift) contrasts with and contradicts the wooden ball (the second gift). In Froebel's notion of a sequence, there is not a smooth progression but slight changes in the familiar, since learning involves challenges to what is already known. This has important implications later in this book, when differences and common features in people are focused upon.

In both the last section and in this, Froebel's approach to the whole and to unity across different aspects of the whole is stressed. Everything relates and connects.

In the same way Montessori's simple-to-complex model can be applied both to her view of the whole child and links within and between knowledge. For Montessori, the links are gradually built, step by step, and a complicated world is thereby carefully made comprehensible. This is carried out through the use of didactic materials, or the carefully sequenced exercises of practical life. She isolates each sense, and develops each independently, baric, thermic, visual and so on: 'From the education of the senses to general notions, from geneal notions to abstract thought, from abstract thought to morality' (Montessori, 1912, p. 4).

In the last section it became clear that Froebel begins with the whole and works towards the parts, whereas Montessori begins with the simple and works towards the complex. The same applies to the way knowledge is not compartmentalised but linked. However, both Froebel and Montessori see the whole, and the way different parts link, as important features in early childhood.

Steiner's notion of unity is more like Froebel's in that he strives to help children towards the essential unity by formulating a network across different areas of knowledge and different stages of development which will illuminate unifying concepts in different contexts. For instance, justice is explored in early education through the child's temperament balanced by activity and imitation. This is done with the help of the teacher who is a mother-figure. Later, it is explored through the history of the Romans, and later still through the notion of justice as an idea, with the Romans as one example of a culture to be compared and analysed alongside others. For Steiner, natural science, literature, mathematics, indeed all areas of knowledge, link and (as seen in the previous section) so do the different facets of the child's development.

Both Froebel and Steiner see links between subjects and between different aspects of the child's development as beginning with the home. Montessori reaches the whole through the parts in a separate environment. Froebel does not stipulate a particular order and method in the way experiences are offered to the child — his later emphasis on play moves him steadily away from this. Later in this chapter, this idea will become important, as it leads towards an *informally* structured interactionist approach to early childhood. Montessori and Steiner, however, help the child towards links within knowledge and unity within themselves through a *formally* structured interactionist approach, with a clearly set down curriculum.

Froebel, Montessori and Steiner agree that the whole and the linkage of the parts to the whole are equally important.

4 Intrinsic motivation, resulting in child-initiated and self-directed activity, is valued

Froebel, Montessori and Steiner agree that children are self-motivating. There is no need for adults to find ways of motivating them. The difficulty lies in that adults tend to cut across the child's self-motivation because of a tendency to be too dominant.

Froebel makes the distinction between play and work. Play is what children are involved in when they initiate the task and work is what they do when they fulfil a task required by an adult. If the child is required to work rather than play, he or she follows a task presented to him by another, and does not reveal his/her own creativeness and inclinations, but those of another.

The skill of the adult educator is in entering the child's play, led by the initiative of the child, as a partner who shares the process. The adult may intervene sensitively (not interfere) when appropriate, so that the child is not dominated by the adult, but equally is not left to flounder. Adults can support and extend children's play. There are moments when children do not require help and moments when they do. The skill of the adult, in Froebel's view, lies in knowing how and when to intervene. Through play, children can actively manipulate, rearrange, act on and reflect on their learning. Adults reflect through discussion, through literature, through writing and meditation. Children reflect through concretely acting out past experiences, or concretely preparing for them. Play helps them to grasp and try out their learning in concrete ways.

So Froebel, through his attitude to play, can be seen to value child-initiated and child-directed activity. He did not stress play as the only aspect of self-directed, self-motivated activity. He also emphasised the arts, natural science, mathematics, and all the areas of knowledge in the curriculum. He saw these as another mechanism through which children would make 'the inner outer and the outer inner'. As seen in principles 2 and 3, processes in the child's development, and encounters with different areas of knowledge, emphasise and affect the child's ability to initiate and self-direct.

Montessori also stresses intrinsic motivation and the self-directed child-initiative which results. Her prepared environment is designed to encourage self-chosen tasks. In Montessori's approach, self-direction is encouraged by 'real' tasks, or apparatus which is based on Montessori's observation of children's natural concerns — for example, the way children love to put objects into rows or to build towers. However, Montessori did not value play. She saw it as an insult to the child: 'If I were persuaded that children need to play, I would provide the proper apparatus, but I am not so persuaded ' (Kilpatrick, 1914, p. 42). She felt that children search for a real life. Rather than toys, Montessori argues:

> We must give the child an environment that he can utilise by himself: and a little wash-stand of his own, some small chairs, a bureau with drawers he can open, objects of common use that he can operate, a small bed in which he can sleep at night under an attractive blanket he can fold and spread by himself (Montessori, 1975, p. 116).

Her exercises of practical life are geared towards real household tasks. However, her rejection of play does not mean a rejection of self-direction:

> To take certain objects and to present them in a certain fashion to the child, and then to leave the child alone with them and not to interfere (Montessori, 1949, p. 253).

Her materials offer children choices of a different nature, within a prescribed sequence. For Montessori, children need a prepared environment in which the complicated world is simplified by means of a set sequence for the children to move through, with the tranquillity which develops concentration. The highest moment is the silence which attends the 'polarisation of the attention', when the child is so absorbed that he/she is not in communication with others. Self-motivation is fed most by isolating children from the world, and its height is reached by their choosing to isolate themselves within the prepared environment which is so designed that they may be enabled and free to do so (Bruce, 1976).

Steiner deals with self-directed activity differently. During the early years, the child lives mainly in the 'will' element, where the spirit is beginning to fuse with the limbs. The teacher understands the temperament of each child. Children tend to be sanguine (calm), choleric (easily angered), phlegmatic (sluggish) and melancholic (peevish). Often they are a combination of these. The teacher helps the children to use their natural temperament for the best. Francis Edmund (1979, p. 61) says of Steiner, 'His golden rule is never to go against the temperament of a child but always go with it.'

In other words, the temperament or intrinsic motivation of the child is considered the self-directing force. Children need to be carefully observed in order to establish the way they are to be grouped in class and what help they will need in order that their intrinsic motivation can best be allowed to develop of itself. Different children require different kinds of help within the stage of their predominant will. The key to this stage is the point when the child actively wants to do things and has the urge to initiate. The right setting for and organisation of this stage for individual temperaments are part of the promotion of intrinsic motivation which frees the child to initiate and self-regulate. By the age of 14, having progressed from the early stage of the 'will' through the period of the 'heart' or feelings to the period of the 'head', the young man/women can self-direct his/her attention towards causes, reasons and explanations. These young people are in a position freely to explore ideas.

Self-directed activity varies according to the different approaches. Froebel emphasises the value of play and language, actions, feelings and thoughts, Montessori emphases the value of real tasks, and Steiner emphasises the different needs of the stages of the will, the heart and the head in relation to this. However, all three stress self-directed, child-initiated activity as aspects of intrinsic motivation. Intrinsic motivation is fundamental to all three philosophies.

5 Self-discipline is emphasised

Closely linked with intrinsic motivation, and with the need to promote it by allowing children to initiate and self-regulate tasks, activities and ideas, is the development of self-discipline.

Self-discipline is probably one of the most important elements in life. Without it, no matter how imaginative, creative, logical, or skilful a person is, there will be no development or persistence to the completion of the work. Froebel, Montessori and Steiner all agree that self-discipline emerges from keeping intrinsic motivation intact.

We saw how Froebel emphasises play as a means by which the child willingly sees things through to completion. This sort of environment favours the development of self-discipline — the strong, confident self with sufficiently high self-esteem not to be distracted from fulfilling an objective, or working towards ideals. Froebel (1887, p. 131) says: 'The faith and trust, the hope and anticipation with which the child enters school accomplishes everything.' The teacher must not destroy this, but through a dialogue with and respect for the child will help self-discipline to emerge, a discipline that is an inner influence rather than an external force.

The partnership element of the relationship between adult and child is stressed. The adult helps the child to articulate and understand events in which he/she has participated through language, play and activities. Inner influence rather than external force is the key to the emergence of self-discipline. Froebel would shudder to see any kind of extrinsic reward.

At the centre of Froebel's approach to discipline is his belief that the child's intrinsic motivation should not be damaged. This is encouraged by his belief that humans are basically good. He rejected the notion of original sin. He says:

> . . . the only and infallible remedy for counteracting any shortcoming and even wickedness is to find the originally good source, the originally good side of the human being that has been repressed, disturbed, or misled into the shortcoming, and then to foster, build up, and properly guide this good side. Thus the shortcoming will at last disappear, although it may involve a hard struggle *against habit, but not against original depravity* [Froebel's italics] in man (1887, pp. 121-2).

In the disciplining of the child, Froebel places emphasis on discussion between the teacher and the pupil in bringing to light this good tendency. Discussion helps the child to analyse and reflect, to come to an understanding of the implications of actions and so to work out a solution to problems. Froebel emphasises mutual respect between the teacher and the pupil. A truly reciprocal partnership between child and adult is central to his philosophy. Froebel's attitude to self-discipline leads towards an informally-structured interactionist curriculum.

Montessori also asserted the importance of self-discipline. She did so by stressing the child's need for protection from the over-dominating adult, thus allowing space for self-regulation. The child who is separated from the over-directive, cacophonic inputs of adults, and in tranquillity is allowed to fulfil his/her individual inner needs, is able to develop self-discipline.

> The child needs rest and a peaceful sameness in order to construct his inner life: yet, instead, we disturb him with our continual, brutal interruptions. We hurl a quantity of disordered impressions at him that are often sustained with such rapidity that he has not time to absorb them. Then the child cries in the same way that he would if he were hungry or had eaten too much and was feeling the first signs of digestive disturbance (Montessori, 1975, p. 127).

There are limits to self-discipline. Montessori (1912, p. 87) says, 'The liberty of the child should have as its limit the collective interest.'

The disciplining of the child is approached by isolating the child who transgresses. Contrary to Froebel's approach, there is no emphasis on discourse with others. The emphasis is rather on harmony through silence and watching others' self-regulating behaviour.

> This isolation succeeds in calming the mind: from this position he could see the entire assembly of his companions, and the way in which they carried on their work was an object lesson much more efficacious than any words of the teacher could possibly have been.

Froebel and Montessori encourage self-discipline in different ways. Froebel stresses play and discourse with adults and other children. Montessori stresses silent absorption in the prepared environment and watching others. However, both Froebel and Montessori agree that self-discipline is of central importance in the development of the child.

Steiner also asserts the importance of self-discipline. Like Froebel and Montessori, he sees it as emerging from allowing the child's natural willingness to learn, to initiate, to create an ability to self-regulate during development. He emphasises the need to have a broad understanding of the world which will awaken human potential. Like Froebel, he stresses the community as a powerful influence in the development of self-discipline.

In a Steiner education the aim is to help each person find his or her right place in life, to fulfil his/her destiny. Self-discipline is a part of this.

In contrast to Froebel's emphasis on conversation and language, with the Steiner approach discussion is not introduced until much later. In this respect Steiner and Montessori are nearer to each other. They see the child as absorbing the environment in the early years. Discussion is not seen as a mechanism through which children begin to reflect on situations in the development of self-discipline. Steiner's children first develop through the atmosphere created by the mother/teacher in the first seven years. Then their temperament is supported, in the middle years, by the authority of the teacher who extends them further — for example, with stories, songs and history. Only later does discussion relating to ideas and knowledge dominate the approach to self-discipline.

Froebel and Steiner emphasise the importance of the community of adults and children in the development of self-discipline. Froebel stresses the need for discourse as an aspect of this. In contrast, Montessori requires a tranquil setting, free from over-dominant adults, or children who cut across the self-disciplined work of another child. Steiner and Montessori stress the way children imitate what surrounds them, and construct prescribed environments in which to set children, where they can be protected from damaging external influences.

Froebel's philosophy leads to an informally structured approach to early childhood. Montessori's and Steiner's philosophies lead to a formally structured approach with set procedures to deal with each step in the child's development. All three give a high place to the need to create situations which enable the development of self-discipline.

6 There are specially receptive periods of learning and different stages in development

The end of the last section leads to the need for some consideration of stage theory in Froebel's, Montessori's and Steiner's philosophies. Both Montessori and Steiner prescribe set procedures to deal with each stage in the child's development. In other words, stages in the child are closely linked with curriculum content and the environment in which the child is set. In Froebel's later philosophy, curriculum content and the child's environment are not prescribed.

Froebel's statement, 'At every stage be that stage', summarises his view. He designed the gifts and occupations to make use of each stage in development. For example, the soft sphere is the first gift, the wooden sphere, cylinder and cube the second, while the occupations include paper-folding, plaiting, cutting and pricking paper, and stick-laying. The message he is giving is to allow children fully to experience within the level at which they are functioning rather than to attempt to accelerate them on to the next stage. He is arguing for activities which are broad rather than narrow and designed only to reach the next step in the hierarchy of knowledge as quickly as possible. The skill of the adult lies in observing the child and, acting in the light of observations, extending at that level (Bruce, 1978; 1984).

'At every stage be that stage' is for Froebel optimised by paying attention to physical activity, aesthetic knowledge (feelings) and scientific knowledge (thought). In this way the child fully experiences each stage. This links with Froebel's view that every stage exists in its own right. Speedy acceleration towards adulthood cuts across breadth of knowledge and experience. A richly developed person is more likely to emerge if children are encouraged fully to experience the stage at which they are.

Montessori's notion of the 'sensitive period' (which she took from the Dutch biologist Hugo de Vries) is probably her most important contribution to the education of young children (Bruce, 1976). Sensitive periods occur when 'an irresistible impulse urges the organism to select only certain elements in its environment, and for a definite, limited time' (Montessori, 1949).

Montessori is very specific about the way the sensitive periods should be dealt with, and here she parts company with Froebel. She lays down precisely, in what she calls her scientific method, how her didactic materials, exercises of practical life, and potters' arts should be used to get the most out of such periods. They allow for the practising of maturing skills during sensitive periods. They contrast with Froebel's more open-ended approach.

Steiner also sees certain stages in development as particularly receptive and requiring certain attention — for
example, at 12 years old Steiner believes it is right for
children to start physics, chemistry and mechanics:

> The time of (this) connection of spirit with the most physical material
> of the body is the right time for the introduction of Physics,
> Chemistry and Mechanics. Thus again we see how subjects are in tune
> with the forces of growth (Wilkinson, 1980, p. 14).

Steiner is more like Montessori in his reaction to stages of
development, as he sets down precisely what is appropriate
in his method. Froebel is less precise about what ought to be
done during sensitive periods, in terms of the exact
knowledge children should meet, or experiences they
should encounter. His concern is for adults to recognise
stages of order through observing a child carefully, and
work out their own ways of acting upon their insights. At
one stage in his life he began setting out more specific in-
structions, but later moved away from this more
curriculum-based and adult-focused approach to his earlier
child-focused work. This was probably because he found
that adults used his gifts and occupations too narrowly
(Liebschner, 1985, p. 40). Montessori and Steiner prescribed
specific action which leaves the adult with less choice.

These different views of how to build on the stages or
sensitive periods lead to important practical differences in
approach which are still seen today. Froebel's view leads to
an indirectly structured approach. This relies heavily on
sound initial training and later good quality in-service training for teachers studying child development and acquiring
knowledge of the subject to be taught. His is an open
system, with incompleteness (an unfinished state) an
important ingredient for ensuring development — with
great responsibility devolving upon the teacher.

In contrast, Montessori and Steiner lead on to a more formally structured approach with a more tightly controlled
programme which does not rely on constant new inputs,
since it is itself a complete system.

However, Froebel, Montessori and Steiner all believe that
there are definite stages in development which require
appropriate and sensitive handling. They all assert that each
stage is important in its own right, and should not be
accelerated, but enriched at that level.

7 What children can do (rather than what they cannot do) is the starting point in the child's education

The idea of starting with what children can do, rather than with what they cannot do, is common to Froebel, Montessori and Steiner.

Froebel's belief in this principle is encapsulated in one of his most famous remarks: 'Begin where the learner is'. For Froebel, play alerts the adult to what the child is able to do and what is needed in order both to support and, very importantly, to extend learning at that stage. He sees play as a mediating factor between the knowledge the child is acquiring, be it aesthetic or scientific, and the natural and spiritual development within the child.

Like Froebel, Montessori stresses observing children in order to see what they can do and to build on this as the starting point. Her approach is based on the observations she made of children, many of them with special needs. These observations may account for the particular emphasis her method places on action and the lack of emphasis on imagination and language. She developed didactic materials, exercises of practical life, and graded sequences to exploit what the child could do, and to help each child develop at his or her own pace in carefully spaced steps. Her three-part language lesson demonstrates her desire to build on success, rather than emphasise weakness. At the point of failure, the sequence is stopped.

> Then in order to teach the colours, she says, showing him the red, 'This is the red', raising her voice a little and pronouncing the word 'red' slowly and clearly; then showing him the other colour, 'This is blue.' In order to make sure that the child has understood, she says to him, 'Give me the red, give me the blue.' Let us suppose that the child, following the last direction, made a mistake. The teacher does not repeat, and does not insist: she smiles, gives the child a friendly caress, and takes away the colours (Montessori, 1912, p. 109)

In order to assess what point in the sequences the child has arrived at, and to use the materials or sequences properly, the directress must be a proficient observer of children.

Froebel and Montessori stress the importance of observing children and building on what they can do, in order to make maximal use of each stage of development. Steiner also subscribes to this view.

In the early years (up to seven years of age), the will is dominant as the child's spirit fuses with the limbs. Steiner's belief in reincarnation led him to insist that the adult needs to build on what the child brings with him/her from a previous life. To do this, the adult must observe the child and assess his/her temperament. Children should be grouped so that there is a balance of different temperaments. If the community (the whole) functions well, so can the parts. In a previous section, it became clear that the part is the reflection of the whole in Steiner's philosophy. In this way, the environment can be structured for the teacher to build on the child's strength by using what the child can do — it encourages physical activity (baking, painting, planting a garden, for example) and allows for imitation as the child absorbs his/her surroundings. The aim is to go with the child's abilities, not against them.

Froebel stresses both play and the people the child mixes with. Montessori stresses specially-designed equipment and exercises used with the guidance of a skilled adult. Steiner stresses physical activity, imitation and the temperament. However, each also emphasises what the child can do now, in the present. All three assert the importance of building on strength because this does not damage the intrinsic motivation or developing self-discipline of the child. Through careful observation, based on knowledge of the stages of child development, the adult can work with the child rather than against what is natural. In this way, children are more likely to be prepared to struggle and persevere when difficulties in learning are inevitably encountered. The message that Froebel, Montessori and Steiner give is that success leads to success.

8   There is an inner life in the child which emerges especially under favourable conditions

The inner life of the child is deeply valued by Froebel, Montessori and Steiner; it features especially in children's imagination, creativity, symbolic functioning and language. Froebel stressed that children need help in absorbing and transforming knowledge into clear ideas, feelings and knowledge. He emphasised physical knowledge, aesthetic knowledge and scientific knowledge, and helped children to take these into themselves through activities, the Mother songs (Froebel, 1878), gifts, occupations, and direct experience of nature (for example, gardening). He saw conversations as an important part of this process. He stressed play as an integrating mechanism (Froebel, 1887, p. 55). Children also need to share these learning experiences, and to use the knowledge they have 'processed' and 'transformed'. The activities mentioned also have this possibility. Children paint, fold paper (the occupations), use bricks (the gifts) and work in the garden. Froebel aimed 'to make the outer inner and the inner outer' though a wide range of experiences.

He stressed play, the imagination, and the ability of the mind to make the 'inner outer', to transform knowledge, 'to associate facts into principles'. He stressed the importance of images through the Mother songs (Froebel, 1878) and through interacting with nature. He says that the child needs help in sharing his/her knowledge through using paint, clay, music, dance, drama, written work, conversation, mathematics and in many other ways. The inner life of the child is fed through imagery, imitation (in the sense of reconstruction and transformation by the child, rather than passive copying), and the child's developing ability in language and non-verbal representation (the symbolic mechanisms).

Physical activity, language, the arts and natural sciences are all of critical importance in Froebel's approach. They feed different aspects of the transformation between inner and outer.

Montessori uses Seguin's three-period vocabulary lesson as the basis of her approach to language work. She drew on Seguin's work because he had achieved remarkable results with mentally-handicapped children and she had also begun her work in education with mentally-disabled children (Lane, 1977). Her use of Seguin's three-period vocabulary lesson, which involved giving vocabulary which is first imitated by the child, then spontaneously produced by the child, does not emphasise the transformational aspect of the inner life of the child in the way that Froebel does. For Montessori, knowledge, as it stands, is absorbed and used. For Froebel, knowledge is absorbed, but transformed in the process and, after acquisition, stored in the imagination. For Montessori, tranquillity is the key to the inner life. She describes her lesson with the seriated cylinders.

> These lessons may appear strange, because they are carried out in almost complete silence, while one thinks in general that a lesson signifies an oral recitation, almost a tiny lecture. . . The teacher never encourages this tranquillity with words, but with her own quiet sureness. Thus, we can say that our own 'tranquillity lessons' are symbolic of our method (1975, p. 137).

The child directly absorbs what is before him/her. The seriated cylinders are copied within the child, and so the outer becomes inner. Language does not feed the inner life in the way that it does for Froebel. Imitation is copy rather than reconstruction. The child absorbs the teacher's tranquillity.

Like Froebel, Steiner, on the other hand, stresses the inner life as the child transforms experiences through the imagination but not during the initial stages of childhood. In the early years, special Steinerian fairy stories present wisdom in picture form, giving instruction and understanding of the world and developing the moral sense. Only later does the Steiner child actively transform the knowledge presented, for the emphasis is on helping the individual to fulfil his or her destiny. What is outer will be used inwardly in different ways, according to the individual's temperament. In approaching the first seven years, Steiner is in some respects more akin to Montessori than Froebel. The emphasis is on imitation as absorbing or copying, rather than Froebel's emphasis on reconstruction. Children speak, sing, model, paint, perform household duties (including gardening), absorbing what surrounds them like blotting paper. Imagination is stressed through fairy stories (wisdom in picture form), but a child is seen to drink in and absorb the environment without at first much transformation. The child needs protection from the world outside the Steiner community (e.g. the wrong colour scheme in rooms, inappropriate toys, TV), and this continues to some extent into middle childhood. In other words, the emphasis in the first two periods of life is on the outer being made inner through absorbing that which surrounds the child. It is not until the last period that independent thinking is considered to emerge and the inner transforms and uses what has been absorbed.

The inner life of the child is directly helped through graded sequences and experiences in a prepared environment by Montessori's method. Steiner also creates a community where the child meets carefully selected experiences, led directly by the adult. Both offer direct formally-structured curricula. For Froebel, the curriculum is informally structured. The adult, using the tools of the child's burgeoning symbolic processes — the imagination, language, objects, people, places, events — works informally with the child, often indirectly. The adult still controls and manipulates the situation but less tangibly.

Froebel, Montessori and Steiner all stress the inner life of the child. Steiner and Montessori are alike in their approach to the early years of education in that they stress children's ability to absorb into themselves their experiences of their surroundings. In the later years, Steiner and Froebel throughout the child's development emphasise the child's ability to transform experiences as they are taken in so that they fit with previous learning, or cause modification in what has previously been learnt. For all three, the inner life is one of the most important aspects of the child's development.

9 The people (both adults and children) with whom the child interacts are of central importance

Froebel saw the mother as the first educator in the child's life — a revolutionary view at the time when only men were seen as capable of teaching children. The adult is a partner in the child's learning, not a threat to it. First the adults in the family, then the teacher, help and guide the child into the wider community. Through play, children manipulate, reflect, extend, experiment with their learning about social relationships, feelings and ideas. The adult is the child's helper, through conversation and provision of appropriate materials, the arbitrator in quarrels, the orchestrator of the child's learning with other children and adults, objects, places and events. At different times children have different needs in terms of social interaction. Sometimes the adult leads and the child follows, sometimes the reverse.

Similarly, the child interacts with other children. At times children need to be alone, at times together. Other children are an essential part of Froebel's philosophy. The need to play together, to learn to negotiate, lead, follow, learn about the results of quarrels, to experience making music and dance as a group, are all important.

For Montessori adults, including parents, are a threat to the child's freedom and so are other children. Her approach enables the child to escape into independence, concentration and tranquillity. The educator organises the prepared environment so that the child can do things alone without help. The best social interaction means lack of conflict, or argument — it means harmony. Language, as conversation or negotiation, quarrels, imagination and social interactions are not given great emphasis except as aspects of harmony.

Steiner, like Froebel, emphasises the adult, peers and family. For Steiner, this is especially important initially, when the child absorbs the moral atmosphere projected by the family and school. 'What is of the very greatest importance is what kind of men we are, what impressions the child receives through us, whether it can imitate us' (Steiner, 1926, p. 22). Social interaction generally is greatly encouraged — for example, through emphasis on songs and imagination (the playhouse corner).

10   The child's education is seen as an interaction between the child and the environment including, in particular, other people and knowledge utself

The previous two principles lead us to the interactionist stance of Froebel, Montessori and Steiner — in Principle 8 from the emphasis of the child and his or her inner structure, and in Principle 9 from the acknowledgment of the external environment, primarily in the form of other people. Froebel's acknowledgment of the interaction between the inner development of the child and the environment needs some justification, because some theorists have put him in the nativist camp. The following statement by Froebel exemplifies his position:

> Mothers know that the first smile marks an epoch in child development; for it comes, not from a self feeling only, but from a social feeling also (Liebschner, 1985, p. 38).

In other words, the smile is not simply maturational unfolding, but is encouraged by the mother's impact on the child.

Liebschner a leading Froebelian scholar, says to those who '. . . maintain that Froebel's model of education underestimates social influences and those aspects we inherit from tradition' that '. . . such an assessment cannot be sustained at the level of his philosophy nor at the level of his educational theory nor at the level of his practices' (1985, p. 30).

Froebel also stressed that education must be based on the natural stages in development. His view of development is that of the law of opposites. The wooden ball contrasts with the soft ball. New experiences challenge old ones. In this way, maturation and experience constantly interact with each other.

Montessori's view stresses the interaction between maturational processes in the child, the experiences the child has and the environment he/she is in. She describes this view in an analogy with nature:

> Many species of palm tree, for example, are splendid in the tropical regions because the climatic conditions are favourable to their development, but many species of both animals and plants have been extinct in regions to which they are not able to adapt themselves (Montessori, 1912, p. 5).

Her prepared environment provides optimal conditions for growth. The interaction is straightforwardly between maturing structure and experience. For her, people are not central. Even the directress must aim to become like the wallpaper and not interact with the child unless necessary.

Steiner's interaction operates differently. He stresses the way that the spirit and the body increasingly interact until eventually they fuse. The process begins with the limbs, then involves the body, then the head. During the first seven years, the period of the 'will', the child is involved through his/her temperament in absorbing the environment through the process of activities and imitation.

Froebel, Montessori and Steiner all emphasise the interaction between maturing structures in the child and the experiences and environments he or she encounters. For

Froebel and Steiner, the people and community are as important as the physical experiences. For Montessori, the prepared environment is mainly physical and she stresses the education of the senses.

Conclusion

In this chapter, we have explored pioneer influences on early childhood education where there are areas of fundamental agreement. The practical interpretations of these approaches are at times fundamentally different. The impact of the philosophy of these pioneers is still felt today, and in terms of moving early childhood education forward these areas of agreement are of central importance. They help us to put into historic context recent developments and research evidence in the early childhood curriculum.

The disagreements are also of enormous importance. They help us to see how, even within a strong tradition, diversity of practice emerges, especially if the 10 principles are to be continually reassessed and so invigorated.

One significant difference has proved crucial. Steiner and Montessori fused their educational principles with their educational methods and content. This has facilitated the practical handing down of their 'methods' through Montessori and Steiner schools. But this fairly close definition of method and content has worked against their absorption into mainstream schooling. Froebel experimented with fusing his principles with a closely-defined method and content, but subsequently rejected this. Consequently his principles became the driving force behind what adults might do with children, but did not dictate precisely what should be done. Nowhere is this seen more clearly than in the curriculum. Of the three approaches, Montessori's and Steiner's are found to be formally and directly structured curricula, while Froebel's is informally and indirectly structured. But all are structured. For all its intangibility, the informally structured curriculum has stood the test of time to a remarkable extent.

This more open-ended Froebelian interpretation of the 10 principles has proved particularly receptive to the findings of later educationists, especially those working for the interactionist standpoint. The next chapter looks at how four

more recent theorists have supported the 10 principles and
refined their practical implementation — in short, the early
childhood tradition reasserted and extended.

3 The Ten Principles in the Modern Context

In this chapter, recent theory and supporting empirical evidence demonstrate that the 10 early childhood principles discussed in chapter 2 still hold and remain crucial for the early childhood educator. Romantic language has been abandoned and the principles now find application with increased sophistication, in the light of gains in knowledge.

Four theorists, each of whose work has an international reputation, have been selected; they encapsulate in their thinking the 10 early childhood principles and together form a context in which to set recent research. They are *Jerome Bruner* (1915-), *Mia Kellmer Pringle* (1920–83), *Jean Piaget* (1896–1980) and *Lev Vygotsky* (1896–1934).

Jerome Bruner, an American psychologist, has had a massive influence on early childhood education and is perhaps best known for his 'spiral curriculum'. Mia Kellmer Pringle, founding Director of the UK National Children's Bureau, whose book *The Needs of Children* (1974, second edition 1980) has been widely debated in North American and Western Europe, guided the UK National Child Development Study (1958 cohort). In this, 17,000 children (a representational cross-section) born in a single week, 3–9 March 1958, were used to gather sociological, obstetric and medical information. It was a long-term, multidisciplinary project. Jean Piaget, the Swiss psychologist, is noted for his studies of children's thought-processes, which have been influential in early childhood education theory and practice. Lev Vygotsky, the great Russian psychologist, has had a major impact on the West following the translation of his work in the 1960s, some thirty years after his death.

Bruner, Kellmer Pringle, Piaget and Vygotsky each implicitly supports the early childhood tradition and aids interpretation and illumination of current research. Each of the 10 early childhood principles could be supported by each of these four interactionists, but that would be a book in itself. In this chapter, a selection of the most interesting instances of support for each principle has been made on the basis of extending the principle and helping with its practical interpretation.

1 Childhood is valid in itself and not simply a preparation for adulthood

Bruner's thinking has moved forward since he formulated the notion of the spiral curriculum (1977). However, it remains very useful in helping educators to make links between what is appropriate and relevant to the child in the here and now and how this needs to have in it the embryo of more complex sophisticated knowledge which will be required later on. He says, 'Learning should not only take us somewhere; it should allow us later to go further more easily' (1977, p. 17).

The spiral curriculum is redefined by Bruner:

> It is the basic themes that lie at the heart of Science and Mathematics and the basic themes that give form to life and literature are as simple as they are powerful. To be in command of these basic ideas, to use them effectively, requires a continual deepening of one's understanding of them that comes from learning to use them in progressively more complex forms. It is only when such basic ideas are put in formalised terms as equations or elaborated verbal concepts that they are out of reach of the young child, if he has not first understood them intuitively and had a chance to try them out on his own. The early teaching of Science, Mathematics, Social Studies and Literature should be designed to teach these subjects with scrupulous intellectual honesty, but with an emphasis upon the intuitive grasp of ideas and upon the use of these basic ideas (1977, p. 12).

A common activity presents an example of the spiral curriculum in action. Finger painting is often an activity in which young children participate in schools, day nurseries, playgroups and sometimes at home. It involves children transforming coloured powder into coloured sludge. Transformations of this kind are later central to the study of science, particularly chemistry. The spiral curriculum enables the early childhood educator to match the child's stage of development with the area of knowledge being taught. In other words, it is possible to teach chemistry to three-year-olds through the activity of finger painting. Bruner states that: 'Any subject can be taught to any child at any age in some form that is honest' (1977, p. ix).

He asserts that if what is offered to the child does not have within it possibilities for future development in knowledge, then it should be discarded as 'clutter'. This is a very useful way to get a good balance between what children need now and what they need later as adults. He looks at early childhood education as a part of life valid in its right, with its own particular needs, and links this to the necessity to prepare children adequately for the future during their early education.

2   The whole child is important

Kellmer Pringle's (1974/1980) theory, which she built on Susan Isaacs' work (Isaacs, 1968), asserts that children have primary and secondary needs, both of which must be the concern of early childhood education. The fulfilment of primary needs — nourishment, shelter and clothing — is necessary for survival. Secondary needs relate to love and security, new experiences, praise and recognition and responsibility.

Kellmer Pringle stresses the importance of the child's health and living conditions as part of development and that the child's education needs to address itself to these primary needs. School meals, outdoor play and appropriate clothing are aspects of this. The early childhood tradition has always placed great importance on school meals of good nutritional value presented attractively, served in a setting conducive to enjoying food and good conversation in small groups. Children in nursery settings should have access to indoor and outdoor activities, with suitable clothing being an important element in these (e.g., for jumping in puddles a child needs Wellington boots). Attention to primary needs has implications for early diagnosis of children with special needs, and for issues such as identifying and alleviating poverty.

Kellmer Pringle's statement of secondary need calls for a focus on relationships which are important for the child. She quotes Newson (1972, p. 37) who considers that every child needs someone in his or her life who is prepared to go to 'unreasonable lengths' for that child's sake. This has implications for educators working with the child in the context of his or her family. It also has implications for multi-professional work because educators are not equipped to take on responsibility for specialist help offered by other professionals, or by specialist voluntary agencies. In taking a view of the whole child, the orchestration of different kinds of specialist help may be appropriate.

3 Learning is not compartmentalised — everything links

Kellmer Pringle emphasises that the primary and secondary needs of children must be met if the child is to develop. She also stresses that the secondary needs are inextricably linked and 'feed' off each other. She emphasises the child's need for love and security and for praise and recognition as part of the early relationships which the child forms. These interact with the emerging sense of responsibility and appetite for new experiences. The interaction is important because the child who is loved may or may not enjoy a deep sense of security. A child may be praised, but may not be given real recognition. Every aspect of a child's needs, primary and secondary, requires to be met in a co-ordinated, non-compartmentalised way. For example, six-year-old Nikolai was working with a student teacher who praised every step in his model-making. After a while, he looked up and said, 'Why do you keep saying "good"?' In this example praise was given in isolation from real achievement — that is, there was no real recognition involved.

Three-year-old Christopher manages to make an open semicircle which he says is his name. This has been difficult for him, and his father praises and recognises the achievement. The father intuitively recognises that this will encourage Christopher to keep experimenting and problem-solving.

Praise and recognition should link with every other aspect of the child's needs. In the following example, two-year-old Rebecca is learning in a co-ordinated, non-compartmentalised way. She is taking responsibility, receiving praise, based on recognition of her capabilities. She is valued in her own right (loved) and secure enough to deal with a new experience. These secondary needs are being met over and above the linking of her primary needs.

Rebecca's mother became ill, and Rebecca carried tissues to her whenever requested, and sometimes spontaneously.

Her behaviour was, fortuitously, appropriate for the occasion. She felt that it had been a success, and when some flowers were delivered for her mother, she regularly took these to different points in the room. Her mother and her friend praised her for looking after her mother so well. She used her ability to transport objects to care for her mother (e.g. transporting tissues, flowers, drinks and slippers). In this way she experienced being kind, caring and responsible. Not only were her efforts praised, but they were recognised and genuinely appreciated. Since her mother had not been ill in this way before, Rebecca was also gaining a new experience — caring for the sick.

Bruner also supports the view that learning cannot be compartmentalised. He emphasises the way different aspects of knowledge must link up in his curriculum project, *Man — A Course of Study* (Bruner, 1972, p. 56). In this, nine-year-olds studied 'tool making, language, social organisation, the management of man's prolonged childhood and man's urge to explain his world.' Bruner stresses (1968, p. 75) that 'under no circumstances can they be put into airtight compartments'.

His early thinking, like Vygotsky's, is no less useful with the passage of time. No one has been more helpful in recent years in arguing for linking and integrating knowledge, so that different areas of knowledge do not develop in isolation. These examples from Kellmer Pringle and Bruner emphasise that neither the different aspects of the child's development nor the different areas of knowledge can be compartmentalised, or separated from a meaningful context in the teacher/child relationship.

4   Intrinsic motivation, resulting in child-initiated, self-directed activity, is valued

Kellmer Pringle says

> Given the inborn potential for development; given the impetus of maturation; and given environmental opportunities of an appropriate kind and at an appropriate time — what can still be missing is the willingness or motivation to learn and make progress. The essential driving force of the will to learn has its roots in the quality of relationships available to the child right from the beginning of life (1980, p. 33).

Thus, while she recognises intrinsic motivation, she stresses early social relationships as the mechanism which harnesses the will to learn.

Piaget's work has a different orientation. He also stresses self-motivation, but he emphasises self-regulation, which he calls the process of equilibration. This process of equilibration has two aspects: 'assimilation' and 'accommodation' (Piaget, 1968, pp. 7–8). Piaget suggest that children absorb experiences into structures which they already possess through the process of 'assimilation'. This contrasts with the process of 'accommodation', during which structures within the child have to be modified and adjusted in order to take in experiences which do not fit into the structures already in existence.

For example, two-year-old Robert had established that wheels are round. This view had been well assimilated through a variety of experiences, but he was then confronted with a long toy caterpillar with squared wheels, which moved along when pulled by a string. This was surprising and novel, and he had to adjust his thinking to take this in (accommodation). He was active in his own learning. Piaget's concept of equilibration (his process of self-regulation), involving both assimilation and accommodation, occurs throughout life. It supports the notion that children are intrinsically motivated through a lifelong ability to self-regulate. A range of emotions is part of the self-motivating self-regulatory process. Assimilation brings with it the satisfaction of recognising the familiar, of repeating and practising. It brings the joy and pleasure of playing. It brings the delight of humour, or the boredom that comes when familiarity brings contempt. Accommodation brings with it surprise, fascination with the new, even anger that something does not fit in with what has previously been experienced. It can bring struggle and frustration. Instrinsic motivation is deeply valued by the Piagetian approach as well as in the different perspective of Kellmer Pringle.

Keeping a balance between children's and adults' initiatives is difficult. There is a difference between adults intervening to help children, and adults interfering. There is also a difference between leaving children to do as they like and helping children to have initiative, develop their own ideas, and make choices and decisions. Vygotsky's notions of actual and potential development are useful analytical tools which help the early childhood educator to encourage child-directed activity. Actual development 'defines functions that have already matured, that is, the end-product of development' (Vygotsky, 1978, p. 86).

Vygotsky sees these functions as the fruits of development. They show what a child can do alone and independently. In contrast, the zone of proximal or potential development 'defines those functions that have not yet matured but are in the process of maturation, functions that will mature tomorrow but are currently in an embryonic state'.

He sees these functions as the buds of development. They show what a child can only manage in the present, with help. This help may come from an adult, or from a more advanced peer. For example, four-year-old Hannah wanted to choreograph a dance and share it with her teacher for whom it was intended as a present. (Her teacher, Charlotte, had been away for a few days.) Hannah has an idea that the dance will be called 'Looking for Charlotte', but she needs to talk to an adult (her mother) about it. She needs someone to listen to her, but not to interfere with her idea. She needs an adult to find appropriate music, take it to school, help prepare furniture in the classroom, ask the teacher to come and watch, and explain the content of the dance to the teacher. Without adult help, her idea would not have developed so that it was translated into a dance and shared with Charlotte. Four-year-olds often manage to draw pictures and give them to people as gifts. It is more difficult to give a dance as a gift without help.

Vygotsky says 'What a child can do with assistance today she will be able to do by herself tomorrow' (1978, p. 87).

Play is one of the most important settings for the development of child-initiated self-directed activity. Play is also a very important setting for encouraging the zone of potential development.

> In play a child always behaves beyond his average age, above his daily behaviour; in play it is as though he were a head taller than himself. As in the focus of a magnifying glass, play contains all developmental tendencies in a condensed form and is itself a major source of development (Vygotsky, 1978, p. 102).

The child acts in the imaginative sphere, creates situations, voluntary intentions, forms real life plans. In play children must subordinate their actions to the meanings of things, and behave accordingly.

Adults need to develop skills in recognising when children need to be independent and when they need help. Three-year-old Anthony, playing with the dolls house and talking to himself, needs to be alone. He is, with physical props, telling himself a story. At a later stage he will try to write stories and then will need plenty of adult help.

In this next example intervention was crucial. A group of three- and four-year-olds playing shoe shops needed an adult constantly in attendance in order to sustain the theme of the game and the roles they adopted. Neelam (aged 4) was a customer; the adult was the shopkeeper. The children began to come towards the activity, watching what the adult did. The latter invited children to try on shoes, addressing them as if they were customers. Neelam decided to be the shopkeeper and took the money, gave change and bills and so on. The adult became a customer in order to make way for her. At one point, the adult was called away — the game collapsed. Four-year-old Nishaan would not let anyone have the football boots and a quarrel broke out. When the adult returned, he agreed to be the shopkeeper again and let children put the shoes on briefly. In this way, he kept control of the football boots, but let other children try them on too! This game was clearly in the children's zone of potential development and needed a co-ordinator — the adult.

Kathy Sylva *et al.* (1980) in the Oxford Pre-school Research Project found that initially three- and four-year-old children find it difficult to play in groups of larger than two when involved in imaginative play unless there is adult support. Sara Smilansky's work (1968) suggests that adults can take a major role in developing socio-dramatic play through paying attention to the role and theme and intervening sensitively. More will be said about this in chapter 5 on Representation. Children need a mixed diet of solo, side-by-side and partner/group play at different times during their development.

This section has drawn out some of the practical implications of the principle that intrinsic motivation leading to child-initiated and child-directed play is important. Play inevitably involves children in self-directed child-initiated situations. The adult's role and that of peers is as helpful partners in both actual and potential development. The degree of intervention will vary in relation to the context.

5   Self-discipline is emphasised

Vygotsky believes that when children are involved in imaginative play they will renounce what they want, and willingly subordinate themselves to rules, in order to gain the pleasure of the play. He argues that in play they exercise their greatest self-control. For example, three-year-old James wanted to hold the Teddy in the home corner and 'feed' him. But he allowed three-year-old Matthew to feed Teddy, because Matthew was pretending to be the zoo keeper. In order that the game could progress he gave up what he wanted. This principle links with Principle 4. James initiated the constraints on himself in the game. He voluntarily and willingly gave up what he wanted because he could see a need — the roles he and Matthew had taken on were protected and so was the theme. Seeing the sense in a course of action through being in a meaningful situation (which play is) helps children increasingly to decentre. Seeing things from other people's points of view by taking another role encourages self-discipline.

6   There are specially receptive periods of learning at different stages of development

Anyone who has been with children a lot will know that at different stages they seem to be much more interested in some activities than others. For example, seven-year-old William was intensely keen on skate boarding for several months, as well as being fascinated by bows and arrows, aeroplane flight paths, sledging, roller skating, BMX bike riding, tiddly winks and ice-skating.

Three-year-old Kate made a model of her classroom out of bricks and junk material. She put the 'furniture' in a cardboard box on its side. She kept infilling more furniture and people until there was no more floor space left. During the same week she went to the newspaper box and spread sheets of it all over the floor. She said she was making a road. She had a pancake for tea and spread sugar, jam and lemon juice all over it with meticulous care and then did not want to eat it, even though she loved pancakes! These are manifestations of what Piaget has called schemes or 'schemas' (in William's case, a trajectory schema and in Kate's, an infilling one). Piaget says (Piaget and Inhelder, 1969, p. 4) that a schema is '. . . the structure or organisation of actions as they are transferred or generalised by repetition in similar or analogous circumstances'.

The importance of the schema to the early childhood educator is that it provides a mechanism for analysing 'where the learner is' and helps predict analogous situations which will be of interest to the child.

Schemas change in complexity as a child grows up. For the first 18 months to two years they are sensori-motor (based on the senses and movement); from two years or earlier the schemas begin to be represented symbolically, and this form is more or less dominant until approximately five years; but from four years or so the schemas become functionally dependent.

For example, one-year-old Amanda paints a line. This is a sensori-motor action. At 18 months, she is calling a line she draws 'Doggy' immediately after seeing a dog. This is using the line or trajectory schema at a symbolic level of functioning. Later still, a child begins to establish the functional dependency aspects of situations. Four-year-old David, having just painted a thick line on the paper, changes paint brushes. He now draws a thin line. 'See this brush?' he asks. 'It's fat. This one's thin. Look!' He uses each in turn and laughs. 'Fat', he says, pointing to the line the thick brush made. He has established the cause and effect relationship between thickness of brush and thickness of line.

Observing the dominant network of schemas of a particular child at a particular time, and the level at which the child is predominantly functioning, helps the early childhood educator to respond effectively during the early years of education. This aspect of Piagetian theory has been developed through the work of Chris Athey at the Froebel Institute, London, while directing the Leverhulme and Gulbenkian Research Project 1972–6, and has been widely disseminated through in-service work, particularly in Cleveland (Nicolls, 1986), Sheffield (Sharp, 1986) and London (Athey, 1981).

Athey (1981; 1980, p. 8) describes the importance and usefulness of schema for identifying the consistent thread of interest that a child may have. This can be hidden from the educator if he or she concentrates simply on the content of the child's interest.

Frequently . . . children shift from one kind of content to another within the same period. When they do this they are accused of 'flitting' . . . and so they might be . . . but they are also 'fitting'! They are fitting various kinds of content into a particular schema.

One of the most frequent schemas for children aged two to five is interest in what Piaget calls 'enclosure'. Athey gives an example of the children in the Project using large wooden bricks to build an enclosure and then using it representationally over a short period of time as a car, boat, taxi and ambulance. In other words, the content may be flitting but the dominant schema is not. Athey quotes (1980, p. 8) the example of Louise and her envelopment schema:

Over several months, Louise systematically explored enveloping space and certain associated schemas. She always carefully wrapped things up. For instance, she wrapped her clay pancake up (it was too hot to hold). She went round covering things up. When she had covered up the windows of her model house she said: 'Now it's dark inside.' She covered a worm with sand saying: 'You know they live under the sand . . . at night he'll be asleep.' She made a small hole right through her 'home' book. Her mother was embarrassed and carefully mended the book. Louise made: 'A sofa with a hole in it'. She wrapped 'sausages' in tin-foil to 'cook' them. She wrapped up her mother's shoes at home and 'posted the parcel' in the rubbish bin, 'the postbox'. When she arrived at school she painted: 'a parcel with Mummy's shoes in it'.

Using different materials, Louise told a long story (on audio tape) about her cat. The persistent theme was the cat going inside and outside the dustbin and bringing what was inside the dustbin into the house and so on. Her persistent concerns had become sufficiently internalised for her to have an interesting conversation about them.

Some of the most frequently-used schemas are enclosure, rotation, trajectory and grid. Teachers and advisers in Cleveland, following Athey's in-service work, have developed a 'schema spotters guide' listing seventeen schemas they have been able to work with in the classroom (Nicolls, 1986). Athey argues for the greater use of schema in the construction of the early childhood curriculum:

It is possible that the nursery school curriculum could be planned along more rational lines if teachers could make the shift from arbitrary 'content centred' provision (tomorrow we will 'do' frogs) to provision based on a recognition of children's persistent concerns (1980, p. 9).

7 What children can do (rather than what they cannot do) is the starting point in the child's education

Vygotsky extends the meaning of this principle when he stresses the need to aim for the ripening structures of potential development, which require the help of adults and other children. He sees a good education as one which stresses what children can do as their capability begins to emerge. Concentrating on what children can do does not mean emphasising what they can do unaided. It means emphasising what they can do with sensitive, appropriate help. Concentrating on what children can do unaided undervalues the emerging competencies.

Vygotsky points out also that, given the right help, children are capable of higher levels of functioning than if they are left without assistance. Children should not be underestimated. In play with other children, the problem of underestimation diminishes, since they can set the level of complexity, control their own rules, and make their own actions subservient to the meanings in the game. They can self-pace their developing abstract thinking. Vygotsky says that learning 'awakens a variety of internal developmental processes that are only able to operate when the child is interacting with people in his environment, and in co-operation with his peers' (1978, p. 90).

This occurs in play when children can operate at a higher level through being supported by other children. Only later is this knowledge sufficiently internalised to 'become part of the child's independent developmental achievement'.

The same applies when children are introduced to new activities, such as cutting with scissors, using glue and so on. Vygotsky states, 'The child acquires certain habits and skills in a given area before he learns to apply them consciously and deliberately' (Donaldson et al., 1983, p. 266).

During play, or in problem-solving supported by an adult, the child is using what he/she can do, but at the same time

Tennis

the game or the adult's contribution will ' . . . awaken and direct the system of processes in the child's mind which is hidden from direct observation and subject to its own developmental laws' (Donaldson *et al.*, 1983, p. 267).

Instruction helps to bring consciousness and deliberate mastery to the child's abilities but only providing he/she is 'within the limit set by the state of his development'.

The aim is therefore to establish 'the lowest threshold at which instruction in, say, arithmetic may begin, since a certain minimal ripeness of functions is required.'

The child who can use scissors competently and use glue with skill, who can wipe his nose, do up shoes and so on, is in a position to make models or go outside when he/she wants. This involves maturation of structures biologically. It also involves partnership with adults, and actually being taught.

8   There is an inner life of the child which emerges especially under favourable conditions

There are two aspects to Piaget's theory, one of which is stage-dependent and the other stage-independent. The emergence and development during babyhood of the 'inner life' of the child, from toddler to adult, can be plotted through the stage-dependent approach. As part of this process, the stages of symbolic functioning and intuitive thought are of particular interest to early childhood educators. However, the stage-independent aspects also demonstrates Piaget's concern with the 'inner life'. The role of processes in maturation, experience, social transmission and self-regulation occur throughout life. In this section an aspect of the role of experience is taken to illustrate the 'inner life'.

Firstly, and largely separate from the 'inner life', there is physical experience which involves direct, first-hand experiences (e.g. playing with water through a sieve). Children find out about the properties of objects in this way, but always relating them to what they already know through a process of simple abstraction. These experiences can be directly taught.

Secondly, there is the fun of experience which leads to what Piaget calls reflective abstraction (Ginsberg and Opper, 1979, p. 210). This involves reflecting on the actions performed during direct physical experiences. This kind of experience can be facilitated but not directly taught. It involves an internal co-ordination and transformation of the actions which are not included in the presence of the first-hand experience. This demonstrates the need for adults to respect the processes Bruner *et al.* (1976) calls incipient intentions, or Vygotsky refers to as being hidden from direct observation. These processes can be facilitated by the provision of appropriate concrete activities; adults can 'scaffold' the activity as Bruner suggests, or teach at the point of emergence of structures as Vygotsky requests. But it is within the child that thinking is co-ordinated and transformed. Adults cannot think for children and transfer these thoughts to them by direct transmission. They can only help children to think for themselves. Thus, to some extent teaching has to be an act of intuition embedded in educational principles. The teacher has to have confidence in offering and organising the prepared lessons. It is an act of intuition because there is not much tangible feedback from these internal processes, especially with children of three to five. This is also often true of children with special needs. The teacher has to rely on clues from the child that the lesson is feeding the inner processes.

The inner life is crucial to early childhood education, including as it does the construction of images, the reconstruction of experiences, symbolic mechanisms, and imagination — the ability to go beyond the here and now. Wells and Nicholls (1985, p. 41) put Margaret Meek's point that, when powerful voices are calling for a movement back to basics, 'human imagination is one of those basics'.

9 The people (both adults and children) with whom the child interacts are of central importance

Kellmer Pringle stresses relationships, emphasising the affective (love, security, praise, recognition). Vygotsky, Bruner and Piaget also stress relationships, emphasising cognition. In Vygotsky's view, it is from social interaction that higher functioning develops.

Bruner has increasingly come to value the adult/child partnership, particularly in relation to problem-solving and developing attitudes which facilitate the process. The Oxford pre-school research project found that 'the larger the adult/child ratio in a group, the more elaborated the play is likely to be' (Bruner, 1980). Piaget emphasises the part played by culture in the process of social transmission. In this way, the child does not have to reinvent that which is already known.

The early childhood tradition is often seen as emphasising the affective aspects of development and Kellmer Pringle is in that tradition. It is therefore important that theories offering a different emphasis are put forward to balance this view. Although Vygotsky puts the main emphasis on cognition, affect is important in his theory. The satisfaction and enjoyment of playing with others, the closeness of an adult/child partnership, are not in fact purely cognitive. The sensitivity of Bruner's adult/child partnership echoes this implicit affectivity. Piaget (1968) is quite open in asserting that the life of the mind cannot be dichotomised into affect and cognition. Everything interweaves. People are implicitly central in his theory.

Thus relationships are the key to development in each of the four theories, and this paves the way for the support and extension of the tenth Principle, which states the importance of the interaction of the child's internal structures with the environment represented by both people and things.

10   The child's education is seen as interaction between the child and the environment including in particular other people and knowledge itself

Bruner states that a good educator is one who can diagnose the incipient intentions of the child and act accordingly. He points out (1977, p. 20) that:

> Mastery of the fundamental ideas of a field involves not only the grasping of general principles, but also the development of an attitude toward learning and enquiry, toward guessing and hunches, toward the possibility of solving problems on one's own . . . To instil such attitudes by teaching requires something more than the mere presentation of fundamental ideas.

Bruner's thinking has developed over the years since he wrote this; he now gives greater stress to the context in which learning takes place and puts more emphasis on the partnership between the child and the adult.

It is not simply a question of assessing where the child is (Piaget's stages of development, with the schema as an aspect of this, or Vygotsky's emphasis on the ripening structure) and matching this to the appropriate curriculum content. It is more a question of seeking out the way the child sees the situation (the incipient intention of the learner). As Bruner (1977, Preface, p. xiv) says:

> . . . scaffolding the task in a way that assures that only those parts of the task within the child's reach are left unresolved and knowing what elements of the solution the child will recognise though he cannot perform them. So too with language acquisition: as in all forms of assisted learning, it depends massively upon participation in a dialogue carefully stabilized by the adult partner. So much of learning depends upon the need to achieve joint attention, to conduct enterprises jointly, to honour the social relationships that exist between learner and teacher, to generate possible worlds in which propositions may be true or appropriate or even felicitous; to overlook this functional setting of learning whatever its content is to dry it to a mummy.

This means knowing what the child can manage unaided during the task and knowing what the child can understand but cannot yet achieve without help. Understanding precedes the ability to perform, first falteringly, then with competence. Because a child cannot 'perform', or can perform only falteringly, does not mean he/she is not ready for the task. A tottering baby is allowed to walk, and may hold someone's hand, or hang on to furniture. A three-year-old may spill cookery ingredients which can be scooped up from the table. Children need to be introduced to areas of knowledge from the start, but through an appropriate environment (people, objects, places and events). Bruner's notion of 'scaffolding' the activity helps the context and the style of teaching to be effective. His spiral curriculum, knowing what to teach, when to teach it, is not sufficient.

His notion of scaffolding the meaningful context helps to organise how to teach. It emphasises the need to link the child's developing structures with appropriate knowledge in a meaningful context with the adult educator as an enabler.

Conclusion

In this chapter, the philosophies of four recent theorists who have had a major impact on early childhood education have been examined. Their writings support the early childhood tradition as described in the 10 principles; they extend the application of the principles and offer a number of theoretical tools which will be given more practical use in the chapters which follow; and they provide a framework against which to set recent empirical research. The next chapter uses this framework as a backcloth against which to set the construction of an early childhood curriculum.

4 Towards an Early Childhood Curriculum

In the last chapter links were made from the past to the present. The strengths of the early childhood tradition remain, although the language of expression has changed. In this chapter, the implications of the 10 principles are used to develop a modern approach towards an early childhood curriculum. This chapter forms a link between the first three chapters and those which follow: on representation, language, significant others, the ability to de-centre, commonalities and differences between people, and evaluation and assessment.

Constructing an early childhood curriculum requires consideration of three aspects — the child, knowledge, and the environment in which the child is educated. The environment is the means of linking the child and knowledge. It is made up, first, and most importantly, of people, but also of objects (material provision), places and events.

1 The Child — Who are you Teaching?

In chapter 1 it was established that there are various ways of viewing the child and that it is a key issue for teachers to be aware of their implicit approach. In this book the empiricist and nativist views of the child are rejected and an interactionist view espoused (as outlined in chapter 1).

Because it looks at processes and structures in the child, the Piagetian schema has been selected as an example of a valuable additional analytical tool in constructing the early childhood curriculum, and one example of an interactionist approach. It helps teachers to identify patterns of behaviour through which children select and generalise in different situations. It helps to make sense of what they do. The work of Constance Kamii (see Ross Green *et al.*, 1971, p. 146; Kamii and Devries, 1977) and Athey's work in the Leverhulme and Gulbenkian Research Project at the Froebel Institute, London, 1972-6, both emphasised the child's structures, drawing on the Piagetian framework.

2   The knowledge — what are you teaching?

Direct experience in a meaningful context

It is now widely accepted that absorbing knowledge through direct experience is most effective in a meaningful context. This approach builds on Vygotsky's 'ripening structures'. For example, Martin Hughes (1986) found that children could add and subtract small numbers in a meaningful context, but found conventional arithmetic symbols irrelevant. Children need teachers who will interpret what the children know (e.g. about numbers). As Martin Hughes suggests, 'The problem is one of creating links between the novel, formal language of arithmetic and their (the child's) existing number language' (1983, p. 209).

Martin Hughes' work highlights the need for teachers to identify what children already know about a subject, and to use this in teacher-set mathematical tasks. However, gaining knowledge is not only about learning to become competent in a subject such as mathematics, it is also about developing the ability to use the knowledge with imaginative vision.

Language and play

Language and play are important mechanisms in helping children to have sufficient command of knowledge to become competent, and use knowledge with imagination. Like Hughes, Margaret Meek (1985) stresses that teachers need to use what children know — that is, experiences in which they have been actively involved. She places great importance on 'first feeling encounters' (e.g. the first time a child holds a rabbit) and the need for adults to encourage them as a key to imaginary worlds.

Gordon Wells (1983) stresses the importance of teachers building on 'home talk' in order to construct shared meanings with the children they teach.

> What schools should provide, therefore, is the opportunity to develop and extend these conversational skills by putting them to use in the exploration of the new ideas and experiences that the more formal curriculum provides. However, this is only possible if at least some curricular tasks adopt a style of interaction which is truly reciprocal and where the goal of the task is sufficiently open-ended for the relevance of the children's contributions to be negotiated as the talk proceeds (Wells, 1983, p. 150).

Play as a part of the curriculum is proposed by virtually every educationist, but Froebel, Vygotsky, Bruner, Joan Tamburrini, Margaret Roberts and Margaret Meek have been particularly influential. As earlier discussion in this book shows, the skill is knowing when to intervene and when not to.

Play is an important aspect of the early childhood curriculum. The skill for adults lies in knowing when to intervene, and when not to do so.

Subject matter

There is an obvious third aspect of knowledge — the content of what is to be taught. There is general agreement that art, environmental studies, literature, mathematics, movement, music, religious studies and science are essential elements in the curriculum. Content related to stage of development in the child is explored in chapters 5 and 6, on Representation and Language. Once again it is important to stress that the starting-point for subjects in the curriculum is what the child knows in order to establish what can be taught next. In this way learning is undertaken in context, but continually extends what the child already knows. Teachers must understand both the child and the subject in order to manage this.

3   Linking the child and knowledge through the environment — how do you teach?

The environment in which children are taught involves the people with whom the child interacts, the objects or material provision they encounter, the way they are helped to develop skills in using the provision, and the places and events experienced. The environment is the mechanism by which the teacher brings the child and different areas of knowledge together. Matching, supporting and then extending is the key to good teaching.

People

People are the most important part of a child's education. Vygotsky asserts that it is out of early interactions of quality between child and significant others that higher order functioning emerges. This important aspect of the child's environment is discussed in chapter 7 on Significant Others. The contribution made by both adults and other children is stressed.

The chapter also highlights the importance of the teacher as the interpreter or translator from home to school and beyond into the imaginative world. Working in partnership with the child's family enhances the teacher/child relationship. This is part of the skill of the teacher in determining 'how' to match child and knowledge.

Material provision

Material provision makes the bones of environment. It gives children first-hand experiences. It needs to be wide ranging, both indoor and outdoor with natural and manufactured objects. Frequent lack of attention to the external environment must come from some bizarre assumption that knowledge acquired indoors is superior to that gained outside. Audrey Curtis (1986) provides many examples of broad material provision, both outdoor and indoor.

Simply providing sand, climbing frame, and a butterfly garden does not mean that children will learn about mathematics, movement, or natural science.

Matching, supporting, extending is the key to good teaching, and material provision is part of this.

It is important not to let emphasis on material provision lead to underemphasis on the child. Books abound on material provision. The important thing for teachers to remember is, how will the provision be used to serve the child, and how will it help the teacher to bring the child further into an area of knowledge?

Interest tables and displays are further discussed in chapter 10 on Evaluation and Assessment. They are an aspect of material provision which requires care. The central aim is to give children direct experiences, to allow their initiatives and extend them, to support intrinsic motivation broadly and in depth. Therefore children must be allowed to interact with the interest table and help to make the displays. They cannot be static. Some teachers have a wall near the drawing/writing area where children can put up their work and mount it if they wish. Sometimes an activity becomes an interest table after it has finished (e.g. cooking apple snow). A recipe book, utensils and ingredients are put on an interest table near the home corner, and children are likely to try to cook, or to touch. In this way the children can reflect on, and use, what they have learnt as a 'practising' activity free from adult domination and after a teacher-structured and led task. In this way, interest tables and activities blend and, as Bruner suggests, lead towards future worthwhile knowledge.

Themes, topics and projects are another way of approaching material provision. In a class of six-year-olds, the teacher suggested that the boys' topic should be flight and the girls' 'My Little Pony'. This not only reinforced the stereotype that there are male and female kinds of knowledge, but the topic of flight was more obviously worthwhile.

However, most teachers who use a topic, theme, or project approach do not take up the children's initiative. They simply decide on a topic which interests them and introduce it. This is more in keeping with a transmission model of education. It does not support the principles of the early childhood tradition.

Skills — how to use the material provision

Developing skills is considered at some length here because this topic is not considered as an entity elsewhere in the book. The key message is that the teacher should introduce skills which the child needs in order to become increasingly competent and be in a position to use his/her knowledge both expertly and imaginatively.

When Vygotsky talks (1978) about aiming at the 'ripening structures' he means that is the moment to teach skills. Three-year-old Sarah was making a puppet. She had a tube, and wrapped a piece of cloth around it, and had found some wool for hair. She was pleased. The teacher realised that Sarah had had to search for some time for a piece of material of the appropriate size. This was a useful mathematical experience and she left Sarah to it, observing the while. She noted that Sarah kept looking at other children using the scissors. She wanted to learn to cut. The teacher got some gummed coloured paper and started to make a fringe along it, showing how she held the scissors. She found a tube, stuck the fringed paper round it and put wool on the top. 'I've made a friend for your puppet,' she said. Sarah wanted to make another friend, similar to the teacher's, which the latter helped her to do, especially during the cutting stage. The teacher extended this next day by having a cutting activity, in which the children could make collages from easy-to-cut materials. Sarah, supported by her teacher, soon made progress in cutting efficiently.

This approach is very different from one in which the teacher sits each child down in turn and 'teaches' him/her to cut, and then ticks the skill off on a check-list. The activity lacks function, purpose and meaning for the child. It does not build on what the child initiates, or is implicitly trying to do. It makes an error into something to be avoided, and there is a complete absence of any negotiations of shared contexts and meanings with the teacher. In fact, this approach is totally at odds with the early childhood tradition.

Skills need to be taught, but in an embedded context, which relates to what children strive to do. The same principles apply when children are learning to tie their shoelaces, cut their food at meals, swim, draw, or practise handwriting. For instance, the moment to introduce correct letter formation is at the level Ferreiro describes when children try to write their names, or their first 'fixed string'. In chapter 6 on Language it is suggested that the first fixed string is the moment when children resolve the conflict between their own personal symbols and those which can be shared with others. At this point, the child can see the purpose of legibility, speed, formation and aesthetic quality. He/she begins to use clear semicircles in drawing and to use emergent writing. This behaviour is an indication of readiness to tackle lower case letter formations, provided the understanding that written forms are made out of fixed strings is also emerging. At this point, tuition will give the child the skill needed to undertake legible, speedy and well-formed handwriting, which will usefully serve the writing process. It will also help children to present work well. Tracing, using templates, or stencils, completely cuts across this process and is contrary to the principle of the early childhood tradition. It is more in keeping with a transmission model of education. Being able to reproduce someone else's idea of a cat by means of a stencil is low-level work. Helping children to use what they can do — draw circles and lines — tells them that they can draw their own cat, unique, special and imaginative. This is a higher-level skill in the child and needs careful encouragement from adults.

A class of six-year-olds had fully established the repertoire of marks on paper which are needed to form letters in the English language. (Some languages use lines predominantly, some curves, in the written form. Written English uses mainly lines for capitals and a mixture of lines and curves in lower case.) This class was involved in a project on the Middle Ages, stemming from an interest in castles by a group of children in the class. Each child wrote his/her name and decorated the first letter. Some moved on from this to write poems which they later presented beautifully. The aesthetic possibilities of handwriting were highlighted in this way. Skill in presenting work and sharing it with others became appreciated.

Three-year-old Paul sat in the book corner. He picked up a book and ruffled it, dropped it and opened it in the middle. The teacher sat with him and opened it, explaining about beginning where the story starts. She helped him to look at it so that he could benefit from the experience. At story time she used a book with an enlarged text with a group of children. She asked Paul to show her how to begin and he was pleased with his success. He liked becoming skilled in the use of books. Lack of skill brings lack of confidence.

Eight-year-old Hannah and six-year-old William went with their parents to a Barn Dance in the local park. Hannah joined in with gusto after initial hesitation. She had in fact learnt to do-si-do at school during country dancing. William rode round the edge of the dancing on his bike. The following week the family went again and this time he joined in. He was meticulous in getting the do-si-do exactly right and would only take part in partner dances with the family, so that he could get it correct.

A few days later Hannah made up a dance at home using a pop song. In it she used some of the steps she had learned when Barn Dancing. The newly-acquired skills were being used in a new dance context, choreography.

Cynthia James (a Haringey Adviser) stresses the importance of equipment being readily available for children to practise their newly-acquired skills. If the woodwork bench is only put out once a week, this is not possible. Children need opportunities in becoming proficient when they are ready, not when teachers are ready. If children only use climbing frames once a week, the 'ripening structures' Vygotsky talks about are not adequately catered for in the environment. Skills are not encouraged and accidents are more likely. This is another reason why it is important that children have access to outdoor play every day. The clumsy child needs to become more proficient in using the shoulder, because the shoulder affects movement of the arms and hands (Sheridan, 1973). The woodwork bench, climbing frames and dancing are excellent provision for this need.

Places and events

Places and events which affect the child are also important aspects of the environment. For example, visiting the police stable, the mosque, musuems, the train guard's van, or the park and shops, being visited by a puppet group, or celebrating Diwali, are all important. The environment is both indoors and outdoors beyond the school. Places and events cannot be separated from people.

The early childhood curriculum in action

The chapter so far has given a broad framework for approaching the curriculum. In addition, certain basic elements in the learning process need to be built in, namely breadth and depth of knowledge and the pursuit of excellence. The remainder of this chapter gives a series of examples of the early childhood curriculum in action which bring out the points made so far. First, Bussis' chart illustrates the active role of the teacher and child if education is to be open and interactive, in the early childhood tradition:

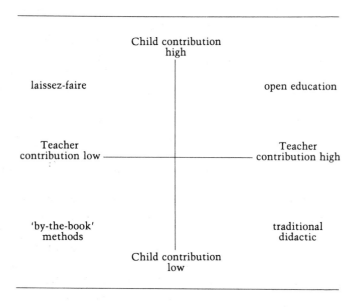

At a nursery school in Southall, West London, a teacher helped the children to extend their mathematical learning. She rigged up a pulley with a bucket and hung it above the paddling pool. Four-year-old Nayam and three-year-old Shazia worked with this most of the morning. Nayam was concerned with filling the bucket before it was released. He focused on fullness, sometimes with water, sometimes with toys he had collected. Shazia, on the other hand, was concerned with holding the rope tight until the bucket reached the top, and then releasing it. Her interest lay in the splash, which she enjoyed enormously. She and Nayam tended to argue, as their concerns were different. With the help of the teacher, they reached a compromise by which he filled the bucket, and she hoisted and released it. The role of the adult here was, as Bruner would assert, to diagnose the incipient intention of each child in order that the mathematics in the situation could be developed. The teacher used the mathematical language of 'full' and 'empty', 'half-full', 'nearly-full' and so on for Nayam. One of the important functions of language in mathematics is that it should help, as Sheila Roberts says (1977, p. 3), 'to describe, refine, and disseminate'. Tamburrini (Roberts and Tamburrini, 1981) points out the need for adults to extend learning through appropriate language in conversation.

Shazia had also shown great interest in the paper aeroplanes introduced by the teacher, and the balloons which were blown up, but not tied, so that when released they darted across the room making a squeaky noise. These were other experiences of hold and release which added to Shazia's knowledge of trajectories. She would repeat the trajectory action of the balloon in movement — showing the teacher with her finger where it went, using words like 'up' and making squeaky noises in imitation of the balloon. This was a mathematical experience.

In a different nursery school, three-year-old Perry's teacher introduced paper aeroplanes, and noted that Perry was fascinated by the vapour trails left in the sky by the aeroplanes which passed over the school. She brought in some streamers and he ran, with streamers unravelling behind him. She was helping him to make tangible a trajectory path rather like the aeroplane's vapour trail.

Shazia and Perry were both using a repertoire of topological concepts to explore trajectories, as well as their 'hold and release' structure which they had had from the age of three months. Williams and Shuard (1976) point out that:

Children notice what are called topological properties first, i.e. not those involving measurement but those concerned with such things as the general outline of a shape, whether it is open or closed or has one or more holes in it, the nearness of one thing to another, the position of a thing between two others. Thus, though distance has little meaning for them, they understand what is meant by such concepts as 'next to' and 'between'.

The relationship between the bucket and the top of the pulley, the throwing of the paper aeroplane, the starting-point for running with the streamer, the bucket in the water in the paddling pool, the aeroplanes landing on the floor and the stopping-point when running with the streamers are all an exploration of beginning and end points, and the relationship between them. The topological notions involved are proximity, separation, connection, and relationships between them, or order. This links with Piaget's notion of the schema. In this case, Perry and Shazia are presenting a trajectory schema — a generalisable and repeatable pattern of behaviour. Identifying this can be valuable in formulating teaching strategies, and presenting young children with a balanced curriculum. This needs to be based on awareness on the part of the adult of the area of knowledge to be developed.

However, although it is certainly true that here is being introduced mathematical knowledge which matches the child's developing competences, these very competences could also be developed in ways which are not purely mathematical. These experiences also contain the 'stuff of dance' (Davies, 1969). The child's structures are there as a resource which can be used to tackle any area of knowledge. The adult needs to be aware of the child's structures, and of the different curriculum possibilities for the child at that stage. The adult needs to bring the two together, as Perry's teacher did in introducing the streamers, or Shazia's in introducing the pulley. Knowing that a child is exploring trajectories is not enough. The adult can extend this exploration using different areas of knowledge, and introducing material and engaging in appropriate language or conversations.

Mollie Davies (1977, p. 3) writes: 'Types of movement-activities in which children spontaneously engage should lead to structured opportunities in the school situation.' The structuring of the curriculum can be direct or indirect, but it is an essential contribution to the child's broad and rich development. For children of three to 10 years old, the emphasis is on indirect structuring of the curriculum.

The vapour trails in the sky and the streamers could be used to make a dance for Perry. Arising from this description of the streamer, his teacher chanted, 'Straight, straight, flutter, flutter, flutter.' He spontaneously moved accordingly, used his body and the space around him, and changed the movement quality from taut to floppy — that is, used the phrase expressively and showed an understanding of how to relate to different aspects as he moved from one state (taut) to another (floppy). The whole thing only lasted two minutes but this was the stuff of dance. It was an indirectly-structured learning situation. The teacher had planned the lesson in advance, but had to choose the moment to introduce it during the school day. A student visiting the classroom that day had not been aware that a dance lesson had taken place, though she watched the teacher working with Perry. In this case the teacher articulated events for her. Often, indirect teaching is not shared in this way, and so regrettably remains intangible to those outside it. Lack of explanation is irresponsible and, in the long term, dangerous. It is irresponsible because the rest of the core early childhood team — the nursery assistant and parents — need to know what is happening in order to act in a way that is complementary. Lack of explanation is also dangerous because it is hiding the light of the indirectly structured curriculum under a bushel. Outsiders can be forgiven for thinking that the learning process is all spontaneous, unstructured and, by implication, not requiring professional 'enabling'.

Four-year-old Harpreet was drawing. He made a horizontal line. He picked up the drawing, held it above his head and, making an aeroplane noise, moved it along in the air. The teacher sat quietly beside him and smiled encouragingly. He said, 'Starship.' She smiled and echoed, 'Oh! Starship, lovely.' He then made a story using what English he could (his first language was Punjabi, which he was encouraged to use in school, but he chose to use English in this context). He supported his story with actions, moving the ship up, down, along and so on. 'Starship go up. Starship go down. 'Nother aeroplane come. Bang, bang. Starship go here [putting it under the attacking plane, which was a piece of construction toy].'

That evening the teacher wrote the story down, and drawing pictures as much like Harpreet's construction toy as she could, she made a little book. He was delighted with it.

This was a story based on the trajectory. Again, Harpreet (like the other children in the chapter so far) is creating his own patterns, relationships, order in the experiences he encounters. He transforms experiences in the light of the repertoire of structures he has available for use. This story could be mathematical (the study of lines, height, and so on). It could be a dance (two objects moving in space and relating to each other, exploding, and so on), but his teacher chose to build on its literary possibilities. If Harpreet had been left to himself, his knowledge would not have been extended into any aspect of the curriculum.

Because the teacher first observed him, and assessed the trajectory and topological nature of his story, she was able to build on his understanding. His obvious pleasure indicated the success of her indirect teaching strategy. Again the teacher is planning the curriculum by building on her observation of children.

Four-year-old Kuang was using a computer to control the 'Big Track' (computer toy). He wanted to push it. The adult showed him that he needed to instruct it to move forward, backwards and sideways by pressing the appropriate key (marked with a direction arrow) and another key (marked with a number) telling it how many paces to move. He quickly understood this, and made it go forward to the end of the room. Then he wanted it to go to the other end. He picked it up and turned it round, ready to go back. The adult showed him how to use the backwards arrow to reverse the direction, but he found this intervention annoying. This demonstrates his stage of development. Kuang could deal with trajectories going in one direction, but not with reversing the direction. He was taken to see trains at Waterloo station. Since this is a terminal, when trains reached the end of the line, they had to retrace their direction out of the station. After seeing the trains he enjoyed action songs about trains reversing their paths — for example, 'Puffer train' and stories by W. Awdry with shunting and so on. He was also encouraged to play games like 'What's the time, Mr Wolf!' in which children reverse in their tracks when the 'wolf' comes. It was six months before he began to retrace his steps in games. Once he did this, he used the reverse button on the computer toy. Computer work does not teach children concepts which they do not yet possess. It is simply another experience through which to broaden what they can already do. It was a useful tool for the adult in diagnosing Kuang's level, and a worthwhile additional experience once the structures of reversing a path were emerging.

The pursuit of excellence involves breadth of knowledge; it also involves depth. Margaret Donaldson (Donaldson *et al.*, 1983, Introduction) points out that a major trend in recent research on early childhood has been the emphasis on competences and strengths in young children. Depth of knowledge builds the child's self-esteem, those feelings of self-worth and self-confidence which are central to the child's development. It helps children to organise, manipulate, control their learning and to reflect on it without fear or anxiety of their inadequacy.

Depth of knowledge is important to the teacher if he/she is to respond flexibly to the child's interest. Every area of the curriculum has a particular pattern, order, set of relationships within it. In mathematics and science the concept of object identity, number and length precedes those of distance, weight, volume and speed. (See Matthew, 1978; Nuffield Mathematics Project, 1967.) In movement, the jump precedes the hop. The hop precedes the skip (Sheridan, 1973).

Each stage in the subject depends on what went before. It is the logical and hierarchical sequences which form a network which makes up the whole area of knowledge. Polanyi (1958) points out that each area of knowledge overlaps with the next, and so links with it. The edges of areas of knowledge begin to fuse as they develop. Knowledge is not static, it advances.

Conclusion

The early childhood curriculum is constructed from three different elements. First, it concerns the child and processes and structures within the child. Secondly, it deals with knowledge: knowledge the child already has; and knowledge the child will acquire competently but with imagination. Thirdly, it brings the child and knowledge together, appropriately and relevantly, using the environment of people, objects or material provision, places and events. The key to the early childhood curriculum is to observe, support and extend.

5 Representation

This chapter looks at several theories, by Bruner, D. W. Winnicott (1896-1971), Piaget and Vygotsky, which help us to explore representation. These ideas form a basic framework which leads to practical strategies for encouraging representation in young children.

Bruner's work is useful because he addresses the question, 'What is representation?' Winnicott, a psychodynamic theorist, makes a major contribution in tackling the question, 'How does representation begin?' Piaget and Vygotsky are helpful in looking at the growth of representation.

What is representation? — Bruner

Bruner (1981) sees representation as the way in which we manage to keep hold of our experiences in an orderly way. He says that there are three modes of representation. First, there is the *enactive mode*, which is based on action. Something is learned through doing it, and it becomes a habit, such as riding a bike, or tying a knot. Secondly, there is the *iconic mode* of representation. This appears when the child is able to replace the action with an image. Images 'stand for' the object. Thirdly, there is the *symbolic mode* which involves mastery of a code — for example, language, or musical or dance notation. Adults need to give children the opportunities for enactive, iconic and symbolic modes to develop, and to ensure that none of the three modes of representation is neglected.

In a sense, none of this is new to the early childhood educator. By tradition, all three modes have been valued. But handing down activities by tradition does not help to develop a framework by which to justify what we do.

Early childhood educators have long believed in the enactive mode, the importance of 'learning by doing' for young children. Here is a quotation from a typical nursery school prospectus:

> The children are learning through the doing, at this stage of development. This means that they will experiment with materials and get messy, very messy. Please do not send your child in good clothes that

can't take glue, paint, mud, cooking mixture, pet food and many activities that we provide.

The enactive mode is based on action.

Early childhood educators also value the iconic mode. Books, pictures, photos and interest tables all keep alive the experiences of the children. Such equipment is an important part of the nursery, encouraging in the children images with which to summarise their actions. For example, it would be typical to find that, following a visit to a pond to collect frog spawn, an interest table had been set up, complete with photographs of events in sequence and displaying equipment, used as a means of keeping alive the experience.

Established methods of encouraging mastery of symbolic codes are also of long tradition in early childhood education through activities such as drawing, painting, making models, imaginative play and dancing.

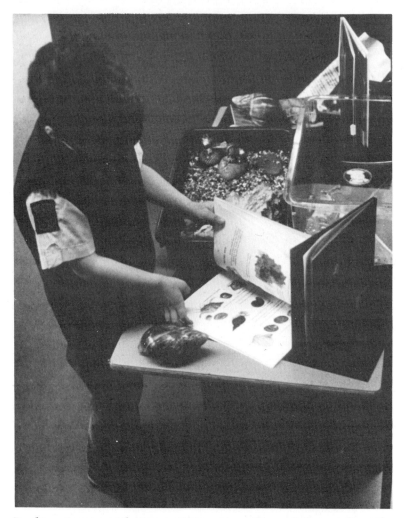

Books, pictures, photos and interest tables all keep alive the experiences of the children.

Bruner's definition of representation gives a broad justification for giving an important place to real and powerful experiences, outdoor as well as indoor, for giving opportunities to reflect, and to use experiences. Outdoor play is one experience which is fast being eroded. Purpose-built schools are being put up with little outdoor space. Outings to local shops and other places are also often regarded as something to be fitted in as an extra when staffing permits. If these are not just a 'frill', but are essential to the development of young children, then they must be fought for and, most important, they must be justified. Bruner's theory of representation is helpful.

His definition goes further than his three modes: enactive, iconic and symbolic. He also claims that there are four characteristics in each mode which support us in creating optimal learning situations.

First, he says that when we represent, we select. (Of course, we cannot absorb everything we experience when we visit the zoo.)

Secondly, we are rule-bound. Nothing is arbitrary, or random. Later in this chapter we shall see how Bruner's work links with Piaget's in this respect.

Thirdly, we generalise these rules. For example, three-year-old Katie draws a circle, an enclosure. She shows a fascination with fences which surround trees in a Royal Park. She selects a picture of Stonehenge from a box of old cards. She makes a clay model of a birthday cake with candles. She draws an island which she saw on a walk by the river. Katie is generalising her enclosure rule, through which she selects from the environment what she will give focus to. (See Figure 5.1 on p. 70 for rule-bound behaviour and how it is generalised.)

Fourthly, we translate from one mode to another. Children are more likely to resolve conflicts and less likely to be governed by superficial appearances (the iconic mode) if they are using other modes as well. For example, the difficulties of putting candles round the edge of the clay cake (enactive mode) are different from seeing the island from the shore (iconic), but the former may help a true recognition of the latter. The island is an enclosure surrounded by water and the cake is an enclosure surrounded by air. Bruner would argue that while the island does not look like an island, experiences of other, similar enclosures will help recognition and help to resolve conflict. (See Figure 5.2, p. 76.)

So, in summary, young children need to have powerful experiences through which to 'select' items for representation. They need opportunities to use their 'rules' to 'generalise' behaviours, and to 'translate' between modes. In this way, Bruner helps us to examine the essence of representation in working with young children. His definition of representation paves the way for looking at both its beginnings and development.

Figure 5.1   'Formula' drawings, simple and complex.

The beginnings of representation
— Winnicott

One of the earliest sources of representation useful to the early childhood worker is the transitional object. It offers a massive opportunity to any interested adult to understand, enter into and help the child develop his/her representational ability in the play setting. Winnicott (1971) says:

> The transitional object represents the infant's transition from a state of being merged with the mother to a state of being in relation to the mother as something outside and separate.

Teddy might sleep with the baby when mother goes out of the room. Winnicott saw the role of the transitional object as varying from child to child. Some children find such objects acceptable substitutes for their mothers. They may rely on these objects, particularly when sad or alone. Others require that their mothers be present if they are fully to savour the objects. However, there is one thing which all transitional objects do. They serve as a link and a separation between mother and child.

I spent a weekend with a little two-year-old girl called Ellen and her transitional object 'Baby Lion'. I had not met Baby Lion before. He is a new friend.

Baby Lion has been taken up by Ellen since her mother started leaving her with a friend one afternoon a week. Baby Lion is truly transitional, standing for the mother who returns at the end of the afternoon, the link across the separation between them. Also, Baby Lion can stand for Ellen, who goes to a friend's house and has adventures without her mother, yet with her once removed. Baby Lion is also Ellen's companion while she is there. He is both Ellen's possession and her creation. The transitional object belongs only to the child. No one else can presume to alter it in any way. This situation has strong links with children's early attempts at writing, which we shall explore later (in chapter 6 on Language).

At the weekend, Baby Lion had a pony ride. Ellen did not. Baby Lion ate lunch and slept. Baby Lion is quite a character, having moods and ideas which have to be accommodated.

Something significant is happening here. Imaginative, representational play is developing around Baby Lion. Other children and adults are willing to have him watch while they play with Ellen. He is sometimes on the edge of games with other children. Sometimes he is part of them. He was taken up a mountain (the stairs) and had adventures. He helped Ellen to find her way into group play with other children. There was a great deal of 'drama' that week-end.

Bruner (1981) says that humans 'select'. This links with Winnicott's theory that transitional objects are selected by the child. Ellen selected Baby Lion.

Another enjoyable time was spent during a week with six-year-old Raymond, for whom the selection of a transitional object varied, its attractiveness lasting for a day or two. One day it might be a camera, then two days later a whistle. Within a few weeks of joining his foster-parents, he began to require a transitional object. It always took him into group play and helped him to find a 'role' for himself. Perhaps Bruner would say it helped him to explore different modes of representation, but in Winnicott's terms it allowed him to do so with safety.

Raymond acted as a defender from wasps on the beach — he believed that they would go if he blew his treasured whistle. He lined everyone up and 'took photos' of them, legitimately controlling a group of people. He experimented with leadership, power and kindness in different contexts and in an acceptable way. Within two days, for the first time, he was 'in the game' with four- to seven-year-olds, helping them to make a museum with their holiday treasures. Although we are primarily concerned with the first five years, it is as well to bear in mind that for some children, like Raymond, the roots of representation come later, but nonetheless healthily.

Winnicott believes that these early imaginative representational plays develop into group relationships and that they are natural and healthy.

Educators of young children need to recognise the major significance of the transitional object to the child and treat it sensitively, in keeping with its importance to the child. By observation and sympathy the adult may be allowed into the world of the child's representational play. This is invaluable in understanding which content and procedures are of interest to the child and how they might be extended through adult intervention. Transitional objects are not a leftover from babyhood, but an exciting development from it. They are the essence of play, which is heavily bound up in representation, and play leads to group work and to representing together, as well as to literacy and other individual representational work. Those involved with young children need to consider seriously how to deal with transitional objects and to welcome them. Perhaps they should not be put away out of sight or access. It is worth considering a special small chair, where the objects can sit when not needed, but are safe from other children. This allows them to be cuddled or carried round, rather than put away in a cupboard until home time. Winnicott would argue that to put the object away denies the child both its possession and its creation. Ellen would not have had her adventures without Baby Lion working alongside her. Adults working with young children need to respect children's possessions, and to be concerned with helping them to create, to represent experiences and situations in a rich variety of ways. Transitional objects are a rich resource of children's representational development.

The development of representation — Piaget and Vygotsky

This section considers how two theorists, Piaget and Vygotsky, help us to explore how representation can grow. Piaget's theory emphasises the importance of imitation, imaging and symbolic representation during the period two to seven years. Piaget, like Bruner, believes that people select, generalise, show rule-governed behaviour and translate between modes. He sees this occurring through the mechanism of the generalisable, repeatable pattern of behaviour (the schema).

Vyotsky emphasises the importance of adult help at this stage, and the difference between what can be achieved on our own, and what can be achieved with help from others. He points out the importance of play.

Piaget, whose theory is helpful when looking at the development of representation, calls the period two to five years the period of semiotic functioning. He says that it has three main facets, *imitation, images* and *symbolic representation,* and that all of these are vital to the development of representation.

Imitation differs from copying in that the child makes use of and reconstructs an event after the event. Three-year-old William sees a friend, two-year-old Charlotte, eat cheese on toast cut into small squares in a grid pattern. He usually has toast fingers. Next day, he asks for his honey toast to be made like Charlotte's. He is reconstructing in the light of a new situation and context. He is adapting an idea he wants to use. Through imitation of this sort, children experiment with different behaviours, roles, ways of painting, swimming . . . This is a strong argument for not separating educational provision for three- and four-year-olds since the younger children benefit from imitating the older, who in turn benefit from the leadership and sense of responsibility involved. The practice of mixing three- and four-year-olds is currently being eroded. Piaget's notion of imitation gives strong justification for the mixing of ages.

Similarly, *forming images* is important. Neither imitations nor images are easy concepts to grasp. They are intangible and internal. Yet the value of encouraging both imitation and imagery is inestimable. Adults can encourage imagery. For example, a teacher, when finger painting with children, might comment that their handprints resembled a peacock's tail seen by them previously on a visit to the zoo. We might add that it also reminds us of a horse-chestnut leaf, or a fan. In this way, we are giving the opportunity of at least three images — the tail, the leaf, the fan — without imposing any of them on the child. Later in this book (chapter 6 on Language) we shall explore Donald Grave's (1983) suggestion that adults need to help children to 'find their own voice' in developing as writers. Helping children to construct images, valuing those they create which are based on their own experiences, is the seed of this.

Four-year-old Dominic brought home a butterfly picture made by dropping paint on the paper and then folding it — still wet — in half. He said to his mother, 'This is like a bird with its wings out. This is like a bull's head. This is like a butterfly. This is like a cloud.' Here is a series of images of his own. This is different from the adult saying, 'Today we are going to make a butterfly painting. What colours will your butterfly be?' In the latter approach, the adult is in control of the images, not the child. If encouraged to do so, children will use real experiences they have lived through as the basis of imagery which they are increasingly prepared to articulate and share. Two-year-old William found some pieces of wood on a beach. One reminded him of a fish. One reminded him of an aeroplane. He had seen both. Similarly, in their paintings and drawings children will often label their efforts because they are reminded of something — for example, a drawing that represented a maze for William at three years of age represented a honeycomb a few hours later. He had recently visited Hampton Court and eaten honey from a comb.

It is important that children should be offered opportunities to imitate an image. It is also important that adults do not offer narrow experiences to children and so restrict the processes of imitation and forming images.

Imitating and images

A student on teaching practice in a nursery school one day took in a model windmill for a group of three- and four-year-olds to make. The children were eager, but needed almost constant help, and the student found herself, in effect, making a dozen windmills. She tried a new strategy the next day, which was still to encourage the children to make a toy as a present for a baby about to visit the nursery. This time, however, she made half a dozen or so different toys, including a windmill. Again, the children were eager, but this time her offering to them seemed to trigger a range of images. They chatted about their ideas, and made a wide range of windmill-type toys although they certainly used (imitated) some of the ideas presented in her model.

Mary made a tube and fringed the ends of it, cutting with scissors. Gareth tore off strips of paper from a sheet and stuck them on to a box he found in the scrap material. Shanaz stood the cylinder she made upright, stuck a stick on it and another across to intersect it.

These children were imitating in the sense of reconstructing and forming images. Both are of inestimable importance in Piaget's theory.

There are two points to bear in mind in Piaget's notion of *symbolic representation*. One is the personal, idiosyncratic symbol, and the other is the shared, interpersonal sign.

For example, three-year-old Hannah decides that a stone is a snail. This relates to Winnicott's transitional object in that it is highly personal. It belongs only to her and no one else can presume to change it in any way. It is not shared and interpersonal, but intrapersonal.

However, shared interpersonal signs also play a part, such as verbal language, mathematical symbols, musical and dance notation — for example, writing your name, saying

'Hallo'. These link with Bruner's symbolic code of representation.

Later, Ferreiro and Teberosky's (1983) work will be examined to demonstrate the way that young children, at a certain point in their development, use the letters in their own name both as idiosyncratic symbols and as arbitrary signs.

For example, Hannah at three years of age used the capital letter H in her name to represent people. The letter H is part sign and part symbol.

Links between the idiosyncratic symbol and the shared arbitrary sign are as yet little explored or understood, but they are clearly very important. (See Figures 5.2–5.5)

Adults can help children to externalise their ideas and thoughts and feelings, so that they gradually want to share them. Winnicott and Piaget would agree on this. Helping children to progress from transitional object to idiosyncratic symbol, and supporting them when they begin to use shared signs, is an exciting and worthwhile thing to do.

Before we leave Piaget, we might draw some links with Bruner. Piaget agrees that children select when they represent. He suggests that they do so through a mechanism called the schema, a generalisable pattern of behaviour, such as the 'enclosure' schema shown below in Figure 5.2:

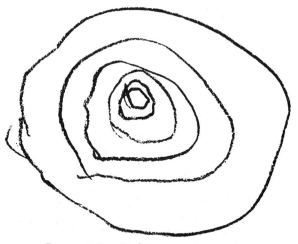

Figure 5.2   Girl 3 years 3 months

For example, two-year-old Christopher transports the letters from the post box to the post office. He also spends time at home fetching tissues from the paper tissue box. He also delights in transporting buckets of water from the water tray to the sand tray outside. He presents a pattern of behaviour — transporting — which he can generalise and which causes him to 'select', focus on certain aspects of an activity. Piaget would also say that dominant clusters of schemas at any one time dictate the rule-bound behaviour which Bruner describes. (Figure 5.3 below shows early enclosure and trajectory rule-bound behaviour.)

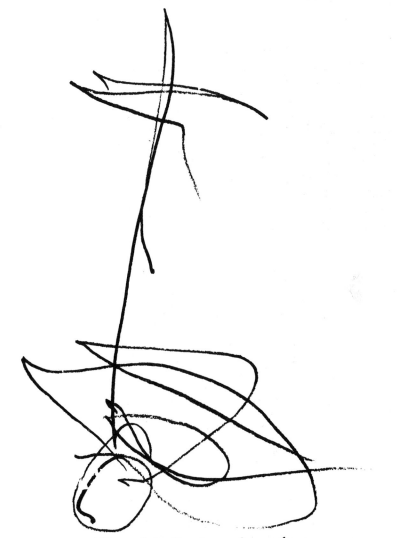

Figure 5.3   Boy 1 year 9 months

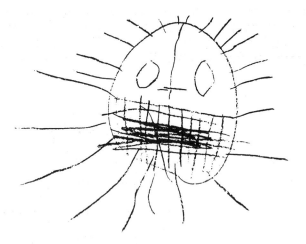

Figure 5.4   Boy 4 years 4 months

Hannah at three years old, as we have noted, draws people using a grid, in her case like the capital H (see Figure 5.5). Christopher at four years old uses a core and radial to draw people (see Figure 5.4) Katie at three years old, with her enclosure schema, uses an enclosure (see Figure 5.1). Piaget agrees with Bruner that behaviours, rules, are generalised and can be translated into different modes of representation.

Christopher at four years old, with his core and radial schema, draws a conker case, makes a pipe-cleaner model of a spider, points out African hair styles, tells a friend what a hedgehog looks like, and wants to use the steering wheel in the family car (a tricky one!).

Children who have experienced making a bonfire and looking at the flames and how they move are in a position to make up a flame dance. Bruner's enactive mode and Piaget's imitation concept link here. Feeling lumps of ice, walking round frozen puddles in the playground, experiencing a north wind are basic experiences which children might use to make music for a cold day. Children who are taken out to see trees, to see a live owl, to visit the zoo, the park, are in a position to make woodland drawings. Imaginative play about shipwrecks could arise from going swimming, or having a bath with clothes on, splashing in a paddling pool and sinking boats in the water tray.

Piaget and Bruner stress the importance of first-hand experience and self-regulation in the representation process.

So far Bruner has been helpful in exploring what representation is, Winnicott useful in seeing how it begins and Piaget useful in seeing how it grows. We need to turn now to Vygotsky to find another dimension to its growth.

Figure 5.5   Boy 4 years 5 months

Vygotsky and representation

Vygotsky believes that when children represent an imaginary situation, they free themselves from situational constraints. For example, for Sadiq at three years old a beech leaf can become a plate. A daisy can become a fried egg. In other words, Sadiq sees one thing (the daisy) and reacts differently in relation to what he sees. He reacts with a different meaning ('this is an egg') in relation to what he sees (a daisy).

This is important. Children seem to be able to operate at their highest level when they are in a meaningful context. Vygotsky would agree, in this respect, with recent work by Margaret Donaldson. First, in a meaningful context, which play situations tend to be, Vygotsky says that children will exercise great self-control, so that the game is not spoilt. They are even prepared to subject themselves to rules which will help the game to last.

Secondly, children when involved in symbolic play will renounce what they want, and subordinate themselves to the rules, in order to gain the pleasure of the play. Vygotsky maintains that in play, they exercise their greatest self-control.

Three-year-old Gracie wears a ballet tutu, and loves to jump in it, enjoying the bounce of the skirt. Her four-year-old friend, Hannah, wants her to walk round in a circle, supporting her while she balances on one leg to ballet music. Hannah is trying to re-enact the ballet *La Fille mal Gardée* which she has recently seen. She needs Gracie in order to relive this joy, and must keep her in the game or lose it. Gracie manages to renounce her desire to jump for a considerable period of time, but eventually Hannah has to agree that Gracie shall jump at the end of each section, so that she is happy to stay in the game. Both Hannah and Gracie are prepared to submit themselves to some rules. In this way the theme (the dance) and the roles (being dancers) are protected.

Vygotsky's thinking is supported by Sara Smilansky. She noted that the three-year-olds in her study in Israel gradually came to use self-control so that games did not break down so frequently. Vygotsky's ideas link with the Oxford Pre-school Research Project (Sylva *et al.*, 1980) which found that three-year-olds operate best in pairs. Only gradually can they manage to keep a game going with a whole group of children.

A group of eight three- to four-year-old boys did play solidly for one half hour on a huge foam rubber mountain (wedge-shaped), perching on top, each with an instrument, singing and chanting, scrambling up and down to change instruments, but in a remarkably orderly way. Four-year-old Gareth was the self-elected and undisputed leader of this band of musicians.

Such group events occur, especially with an age mix from three to five, or even better three to seven, years. It is less usual than pair play, and adults often interfere before it finds its focus, as it appears to be purposeless and potentially rowdy and disorderly in its early stages. Allowed to self-regulate, with adults encouraging it by adjusting furniture or equipment to enable it to develop safely, it can move forward to a high level of imaginative work.

Vygotsky suggests that it is important to encourage this kind of imaginative work since by the time children reach the five to 11 years stages it can develop into rich drama improvisations, jazz, orchestras, choirs, pop groups, dance groups, group collages in art work, and aptitude for planning events in groups.

Vygotsky's work is useful in pointing out the value of play in representation. He believes self-regulation to be important. He also points out that there is a difference between actual development and potential development. Actual development only shows us what a child can do alone without help. Potential development shows us what the child is capable of tomorrow, but he (she) needs the help of a more advanced peer or an interested adult if real progress is to be made. Vygotsky says that play is the ideal way to encourage the structures which are just emerging, which will be the structures of tomorrow. He writes:

> In play, the child always behaves beyond his average age, above his daily behaviour. In play, it is as if he were a head taller than himself (1978, p. 102).

This gives new meaning to the tradition in early childhood education that play is the child's work. It shows us that the adult must be skilled in supporting the play without dominating it, and avoid damaging the process of self-regulation.

The theories of Bruner, Winnicott, Piaget and Vygotsky lead us to some practical strategies. We have established that children need direct, powerful, emotional experiences, and a consistent environment which offers diverse, enrich-

ing opportunities. Young children require a supportive setting in which imaginative play is encouraged, through
which there is also frequent opportunity to reflect.

Some practical strategies for encouraging the development of representation

Observing children

In order to use rewarding and efficient strategies with young
children, adults need first to observe and identify what
children are doing.

A study by Bennett and Desforges (1984) helps us to see
the importance of careful observation. Teachers in this
study had a strong tendency to decide what task they were
setting children, and to 'go for it' regardless of whether or
not the children were coming along with them. They found
it difficult to look at the child in relation to the task. Instead, they centred on the task, and on getting the child to
master it. They often demanded huge leaps forward in the
children's understanding as the task progressed. Careful
child observation, careful identification of where children
are in their understanding (in the process), rather than
focusing on performance (the product), would overcome
this inefficient way of going about things.

However, it is easy to tell teachers what they do 'wrong'.
Concentrating on errors is unlikely to help — the focus
needs to be on developing positive and successful ways of
working with children. Careful child observation comes
first, as illuminated by Matthews (1983) or, using a very different perspective, Strauss (1978), so that the emphasis is
on looking at and identifying what the child can do, before
leaping into action. Bruner *et al.* (1976) believe that adults
need to develop observational skills so that they are able to
'diagnose the incipient intention' of the learner. Adults
working with children will also need to act on their observations of children.

Material provision

Material provision involves people, events and objects with
which the children interact. It can be set out in many ways
to excite curiosity and surprise, and yet there must be

security for the children. There need to be some anchor areas, always in the same places and forms, such as the book corner and home corner. Other areas might change regularly, and link with recent experiences of the children — for example, a Tudor Manor might be created to fit with a visit to the Tower of London.

Different kinds of provision make different demands. Children need to experience the challenge of many different experiences, and of wide-ranging provision. At three years old Hannah danced a rosebud unfurling, her idea. She was very frustrated when she tried to draw this event.

It is important to bear in mind Bruner's three modes of representation, and the conflicts the child must resolve between them. This implicitly argues for a rich, wide range of media for young children to experience and work with. Children need to become proficient in the representational possibilities of different clays, doughs and woodwork as well as Plasticine, mud and wet sand. They need different

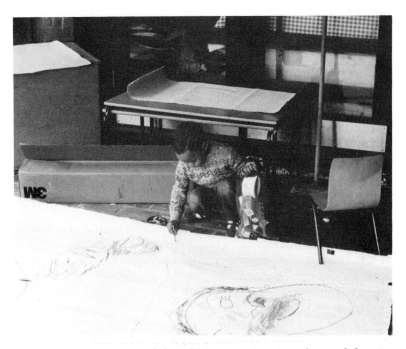

Drawing, painting, model making, imaginative play and dancing encourage symbolic behaviour in young children.

papers, brushes and paints, from oil to poster to powder paint, thick, thin and medium. They need to draw with pastels, charcoal, pencils, felt pens, chalks, inks and so on. A broad material environment becomes very exciting to provide. Children need to experience and tell stories, hear and see and make music and dance in different styles, dramatic, comforting, romantic, folk, from different cultures. Endless possibilities emerge.

Some children will show more strength in one area, less in another. Others will be all-rounders.

William at three years old almost never paints, although the opportunity is constantly available. He rarely draws, either. He rejects dough and clay. But he models a blackbird out of Plasticine, with a black body, head, wings, a yellow beak, two yellow eyes, and yellow legs and feet. He is angry when it will not stand up, and only grudgingly accepts the suggestion that it could sit on a nest made by a helpful adult. He wants it to hop. The representation of movement is what he really wants. He knows that blackbirds have a springy hop. He represents this with his body, briefly, before a rough and tumble game develops with his sister. William prefers to represent using three dimensions, and through dancelike movements.

Kate at three-and-a-half years rarely drew or painted, but made marvellous models. She made a model of her school classroom one day with a cardboard box, and bricks to represent furniture, accurately placed spatially.

Interestingly, at five years old both these children were doing meticulous and beautiful drawings and two-dimensional work, but both were easily frustrated if their efforts did not work out. It is easier to change clay or bricks, and reorganise them, than it is to change a drawing that has not gone according to plan. On the other hand, it is easier to fall into a stereotyped and narrow formula in drawings, and to let dancelike, musical and three-dimensional work atrophy as the imagination increasingly fails.

Representation, in all its forms, is important. Dance, music, sculpture, construction toys, drawing, painting, literature and drama all offer different possibilities. Each offers something special, something worthwhile and unique.

Returning to Bruner's definition of representation, we can conserve events, situations, and objects by many means.

People are part of the material provision

Rich material environment involves interacting with physical material and objects. It also involves people, events and situations. Earlier in the chapter, the advantages of younger and older children playing together was emphasised. Vygotsky's and Piaget's work show how important it is for younger children to see older children handling materials with confidence and pleasure, and to see moments of struggle and recognise how the adults in the environment are supportive and enabling at such times. Motivation to learn and move forward are closely linked with security, self-confidence and self-esteem. This leads adults to evolve skills in helping children to develop in these ways.

Joan Tamburrini (Roberts and Tamburrini, 1981) writes about an 'extending style' in working with young children. In this model, the adult first observes the child's themes of play, drawing, models, conversations and so on, then attempts to help children, individually, to elaborate these themes. This might be through conversation, through suggestion, or by providing relevant and appropriate materials and experiences in a sensitive way. There is, as Tamburrini suggests, all the difference between intervening sensitively and appropriately, and interfering, which is the problem Bennett and Desforges (1984) met when teachers 'taught' before they observed.

Working with young children, providing appropriate materials and experiences, might also mean that adults need to allow themselves to be used as an extension of the child — for example, holding the sticky tape while children cut it, to stop them from giving up at a difficult moment, or helping to keep a theme going in the home corner when the play is breaking down.

Two three-year-olds, Barbara and Clare, wanted to play nurses, but a quarrel broke out over who should give out the medicine. The adult intervened, saying, 'I am the sister. Nurse Barbara, would you take the patient's temperature? Nurse Clare, please would you wash the patient?'

Both are given attractive nurselike tasks. The adult has kept the theme and the roles going, which Sara Smilansky suggests is important. The adult has also extended the children's play in adding to the range of nurselike activities.

Adults can also extend play by encouraging self-regulation wherever possible. If the home corner has a limit on numbers ('Four children play here') it does not allow for Aunty Flo to come and visit, or for games like 'The Seven Little Goslings' to be explored, or for all the patients in the hospital ward to lie down on pretend beds. Through providing various smaller 'dens', as the Oxford studies (Sylva *et al.*, 1980) suggest, play can be redirected to other spaces in the environment in a positive way.

Joan Tamburrini (1982) emphasises that effective teaching strategies in the early childhood years are vital, and that 'direct' teaching is only one form of teaching. Indirect methods, less obvious, less tangible, but properly organised, are an important part of work with young children.

What we have explored so far

In this chapter some of the many facets of representation have been explored. An attempt has been made to define what representation is, using Bruner's theory. We have tried to see how it begins, using Winnicott's theory. We have attempted to get to grips with how it grows, using Piaget's and Vygotsky's theories. This has led to a consideration of the adult's role.

Representation needs a major emphasis in the early years, because it involves us in valuing both the commonalities between humans and the uniqueness of every human. The importance of the transitional object in the early stages of representation was identified. Perhaps a transitional object should have the last say in this Chapter. Winnie the Pooh, a transitional object of the real-life Christopher Robin, and his friend Piglet emphasise both what is common to us all (getting up in the morning) and the unique way we each respond to that event (Milne, 1926).

> 'When you wake up in the morning, Pooh,' said Piglet at last, 'what's the first thing you say to yourself?'
> 'What's for breakfast?' said Pooh. 'What do *you* say, Piglet?'
> 'I say, I wonder what's going to happen exciting *today*?' said Piglet.
> Pooh nodded thoughtfully.
> 'It's the same thing,' he said.

6 Language

Language is about communication; communication with self and communication with others. It helps people to move from the here and now to the past, into the future and into alternative worlds. It uses agreed signs which evolve to fit the times and setting in which the language is used. It enables people to think and feel at an abstract level about ideas which are hypothetical and imaginary in effective, efficient, deep and moving ways. It normally involves talking and listening; it can involve reading and writing. In Western culture all four elements are important areas of language in the school setting and in life generally. To be illiterate sets people at a disadvantage. To be unable to talk or listen cuts people off and brings loneliness and frustration along with the lack of opportunity to communicate with others. Language does not have to be oral. It can be 'talked' or 'listened to' in different ways. Some deaf and blind people talk and listen through touch. The language of the deaf has gained recognition as an official language. British Sign Language (BSL) and American Sign Language (ASL) are not oral — they combine gesture, agreed and shared signs with finger spelling. The work of researchers like Mary Brennan (1978) has helped those who use oral language to appreciate that sign language has a syntax and has evolved just as any living language has, has regional dialects and enables abstract thinking. It contains features shared by verbal languages. It facilitates thinking, feeling and communication. It allows those who understand it to construct shared meanings together. However, like some other languages in the world, it has no written form and so cannot be read.

Recent thinking, typified by Silvana Wiles (1981) and Barry McLaughlin (1980), in relation to children whose mother tongue is not English has led to new views on the acceptance of mother tongue use in schools. Wiles argues that if children are allowed to use their own language at home and in school, they seem to make better progress in the new language they are acquiring. In this way bilingualism can be actively encouraged. Many schools now make provision for children to meet different teachers, some who speak their mother tongue (e.g. Punjabi, Welsh, Urdu and so on) and some who speak the dominant language of the country — in this case, English. This benefits the children who are acquiring a new language in school. It also benefits children who already use the main language of the school but have never heard other languages before. This dual approach promotes respect for other languages and cultures; it also values them and sees them as an important contribution to the school. Far from holding children back, it seems to advance the learning taking place in schools, both for the children acquiring the new language and for those meeting new languages as a broadening experience. The importance of such broadening experiences has been emphasised throughout this book.

It is more difficult for children using dialects to acquire a language which is very similar to their own. These children are often seen as being unable to speak properly. They need the same opportunities as those using very obviously different languages, so that they too are bilingual. Dialects enrich.

Encouraging language

Gordon Wells and John Nicholls (1985, p. 18) stress an interactionist approach to language acquisition which is very much in tune with the early childhood tradition. They argue that language acquisition and development is encouraged by four factors. First, there needs to be a partnership between child and adult. Second, children need to be active in their own learning. Third, it is important that children should be allowed to make errors. Fourth, there is a need to negotiate shared meanings through discussion.

Adult/child partnerships

Wells and Nicholls (1985, p. 18) stress 'the importance of a collaborative rather than a directive style of interaction'. They found that collaborative parents tend to be more successful in building a sensitive partnership which promotes and facilitates language development. These findings are reiterated by B. Tizard and M. Hughes (1984). Gordon Wells's work helps teachers to develop better strategies into the areas of knowledge in which they wish them to become involved. Parents do not have the problem that teachers have. They are not paid to try to initiate and involve children actively in new knowledge. They might succeed in this, but their professional reputation does not depend upon it. The work of Gordon Wells values the role of teachers in trying to help children become competent and involved in different areas of knowledge. He points out that the teacher needs to be skilled in discerning what the child knows and using that to lead into a task, activity, or experience.

A group of seven-year-olds was going round a stately home. The guide wanted to talk about the ceramics. The teacher sensed that this held no interest for the class. She did know about some of the paintings and asked the children to look at a painting of a lady. She asked what Zoe, Mark and the picture had in common. The situation changed, from a monologue by the guide to suggestions from the children with the teacher acting as chairperson. Eventually, it was established that Zoe and Mark had both recently acquired baby sisters. The children wondered if that was the link. Had the lady just had a baby? In fact, the fine lady in the painting had founded a maternity hospital for the poor. The children asked about her — why she did this, who she was. This teacher had taken the children into history and helped them to glimpse the social order of a different time from their own. The language introduced was rich but welcomed. The teacher had helped to establish a partnership by starting from something which the class found interesting and relevant. Her share of the partnership was achieved — it was to link up with a project on Victorian Britain, including the contrast between wealth and poverty, and the social order of the times.

Adult/child partnerships are an important aspect of language development. But so are conversations between children. Children are very good at tuning in to each other, and often a child will 'translate' to an adult what another child means. Parents are also able to signal teachers about events and situations which will help the communication between child and teacher. Similarly, teachers can promote the parent/child relationship by telling parents what was done in school and inviting them in to show them.

Three-year-old Richard was met each day from nursery class by his mother. The teacher made a point of suggesting that, if parents were not in a rush, their child could show

them round. In this way parents had an idea of the activities, models, paintings and so on in which their child was
involved. Later, at home, when Richard referred to a dead
worm, his mother did not have to puzzle over his meaning.
She knew that he was studying newts in school and that
worms were fed daily to them. When, in school, Richard
talked about 'my yellow one', the teacher knew that he had
a new Teddy bear because his mother had mentioned it.

Conversation can be effectively developed to deal better
with situations and ideas removed from their immediate
contexts if parents and teachers work together. As children
grow they can be helped to become aware of the need to explain and fill in necessary information in order to bring
meaning to those who were not present. Listening to stories,
reading and writing facilitate this process. There are strong
links with the ability to decentre in the development of a
sense of 'audience'.

The need for children to be active in the learning process

The second of the four important areas put forward by Wells
and Nicholls (1985, p. 18) is that children are active in their
learning. They emphasise 'the active nature of effective
learning as children form and test hypotheses about the experiences they encounter both in and out of school'.

Children need to have opportunities to initiate conversations in the school setting during activities and during
group times. They also need individual and small group settings — for example, when involved in music, dance, or
story. In these settings they can interject and the adult can
use these interjections to make the story meaningful at a
deeper level.

'I've got one of these' may seem an egocentric response by
four-year-old Jason to the story of *Titch* by Pat Hutchins.
However, it tells the teacher that Jason knows about a pin-
wheel. He explains how it goes round if you blow on it. He
wants to abandon the story at this point and talk about his
pin-wheel instead. The teacher can let him talk with her
because it is a small group of six children. The other
children bring in information about how the pin-wheel
works. When the teacher has taken each child's initiations
about the subject, she takes them back to the text. Jason
often returns to this story, provided it is in the book corner.

Old favourites are an important part of leading towards reading.

Margaret Meek (1985) sees the way children tackle books as an 'active' search for personal meaning. She stresses the 'first feeling encounter' as a powerful experience with lasting impact. If the teacher had not allowed interruptions as she read the story, she would have been in danger of, as Margaret Meek puts it, 'editing out' the memory of the intense 'first feeling encounter' and Jason's initiative would not have been given legitimacy by the teacher. These early experiences with books are part of the 'set towards literacy' which Holdaway (1979) describes. Children bring their understanding of experience they have had and their knowledge of language when they begin to read. As Kenneth and Yetta Goodman say (1977, p. 137):

> Reading is not just knowing sounds, words, sentences and the abstract parts of language that can be studied by linguists. Reading, like listening, consists of processing language and constructing meanings.

Children are active in their learning and need to be encouraged in this. Their active feelings affect their active thinking. One deep, powerful experience is better than many pedestrian ones.

Six-year-old Tom's mouse died. He was very upset. A story about a mouse and his experiences in a cage, and how he runs away leaving his owner sad, contains in it some of Tom's grief. He loved the story. It evoked the memory of a first feeling encounter. Tom did not choose the story — his mother did, recognising the importance of the death of his mouse. Adults need to choose books for children which help them to meet and extend both powerful and everyday experiences. Sometimes these will arise spontaneously, as with Jason and the pin-wheel. Sometimes they need to be planned by the adult, as with Tom. Children relate their own experiences to those of others through books, shared activities and outings, provided that adults allow them to be active in the process. Sometimes the child initiates, sometimes the adult, but the child must always be allowed to be active. Margaret Meek (1985, p. 43) stresses the need to 'foreground the emotive' in this process. She sees emotion as an integrating force in children's experiences. As well as listening to stories and being helped to interact with the text, children produce nonsense rhymes and jokes which she sees as a very important aspect of their being active in their language development. In this way, she asserts, children 'redefine what counts as common sense'. Chukovsky (1963) also noted the need children have to create rhymes and nonsense words which are ridiculous — in other words, the need to be active.

Piaget sees playing with ideas and making jokes as the highest level of understanding. Helping children develop a sense of humour was one of the central aims of Chris Athey's project, 1972–6. Having fun with language, or with any area of knowledge, implies good understanding and can be used as a means of assessing what children know well.

Rearranging ideas and words is the basis of the creative process. Talking and listening, partnerships and being active in language development, lead into literature. Peter McKeller (1957) defines the imagination as the rearrangement of past experience in new and fascinating ways.

The importance of making errors free from criticism

Wells and Nicholls (1985, p. 18) argue for 'the value of errors, to learners as elicitors of helpful feedback and for teachers as a source of insight into the meanings that their pupils are making'. In talking, children are attempting actively to formulate the rules of language. They hypothesize — for example, 'I hitted the ball.' If adults reply by extending, 'Oh, you hit the ball, did you?', they give the correct form without rejecting what the child said. This helps children to adjust their 'rules' for themselves. Direct correction of children's speech is ineffective and may create stress — for adults as well as children! Self-correction is an important strategy as children check for meaning. It also tells adults where children are in their development.

The negotiation of shared meanings

Wells and Nicholls (1985, p. 18) suggest that 'the developmental thrust that adults (parents and teachers) provide when they are prepared to negotiate the shared construction of meaning' enhances the learning of language.

Three-year-old Luckdeep sat down for story time when the teacher told the story of Mrs Wishy Washy and kept saying, 'In there.' The teacher wanted to respond but did not understand. Sandeep explained that Luckdeep wanted the teacher to put the scrubbing brush in the bowl to make soap bubbles. The shared context was not enough. It was necessary to negotiate a shared meaning, too. The teacher then built the bubbles into the story. This links with a pattern of child-rearing which is most successful — the democratic abrasive model. In this approach, children are encouraged to put their views and to argue their case as do the parents. The latter take up children's initiatives, but are still in control in that they make the final decisions. In the school context, the teacher listens to what the child says and uses it in helping the child to go more deeply into areas of knowledge. The teacher makes decisions about what knowledge will be introduced and how.

In this section, four points have been stressed, drawing on the work of Gordon Wells. These are: the importance of partnership; children being active in their own learning; valuing errors; and negotiating. They are equally important in the section on reading and writing that follows.

Reading

The importance of being read to cannot be overemphasised. It was stressed in the Bullock Report (DES, 1975) and more recently in research typified by Shirley Brice Heath (1983), Henrietta Dombey (1983) and Caroline Fox (1982). The bedtime story is one important way in which, in a one-to-one situation, an adult can give meaning to the text. Dorothy Butler (1980) stresses that even babies can appreciate books. By looking at books in this way, adults can take up children's initiatives, giving and extending the meaning in them. Children begin to meet different worlds with the adult as translator.

A dance group called 'Janet Smith and Dancers' choreographed *Winnie the Pooh*. Throughout the performance children in the audience were asking their parents, 'Who's that? What's she doing?' and so on. Adults were constantly translating and interpreting the performance for the children. Every so often, children would cry out joyously, 'That's the Woozle!' as they recognised the stories read to them at home from a book. A puppet show of an African tale had a similar effect with children aged four to seven. Shared experiences like these are important in enabling children to grasp what is involved in formal book language. Pictures, dancers, puppets, and songs help book language to develop.

Don Holdaway (1979) stresses the importance of chants and song as the basis of 'storying'.

Knowing a story well — the old favourites — helps children to predict when they read. Reading is largely prediction. Children need to understand about syntax, semantics and grapho-phonic aspects of texts in order to read. Their own knowledge of language, the way they have 'cracked the language code', will enable them to tackle syntax in a text. Kenneth and Yetta Goodman believe that 'reading involves the relationship of all the language systems (1977, p. 142)'. When children begin to read, the Goodmans assert that they are 'using their knowledge of language and their conceptualisation to get meaning from print (p. 133)'.

Being read to is centrally important. Listening to stories with a rich variety of texts helps children to learn about words and sentence structures in book language. The intentions children have about meanings, the way they bring their own experiences to bear, enables this process (Goodman, 1980). The more help they have had in using language with others in a meaningful way, and in using understanding of book language and its ability to created what Margaret Meek calls 'possible worlds', the better.

The grapho-phonic aspect (how it looks and sounds) develop in synchrony with syntax and semantics. Just as vocabulary-building does not lead to rich language development, so rote teaching of letter shapes, or teaching phonics out of context, do not promote efficiency and understanding of word and letter blends, or word-building. The meaningful context best promotes the teaching of each of these areas. Don Holdaway (1979) stresses individual reading to and with a child. He also advocates the use of enlarged texts in 'shared books' for group story times, when discussion of graphophonic aspects can be included in an unstressful setting. In this way children establish that the letter 'a' in the alphabet is consistently written in one way, in contrast to its phonic aspect (e.g., the 'a' in 'hat' is pronounced differently from the 'a' in 'hate'). Putting stories on to cassettes, and encouraging children to listen to them through headsets while following in the book, is an activity often referred to as 'Listening Post'. This type of work gives further variety and helps the auditory aspect of reading. These are some ways in which children can be helped to move from picture books to reading the text, both at home and in school. Liz Waterland says the situation is *not* one where it is:

> assumed that the child will be doing all the reading with the adult in some sense sitting in judgement, noting miscues, giving direct teaching or asking comprehension-testing questions. I have, however, already described the approach we wish to adopt as a craftsman/ apprentice relationship in which the adult demonstrates the craft and supports the children in whatever contibution they are able to make (1985, p. 29).

The central factor is building up shared contexts and meanings in relation to print. The adult helps the child to construct meaning with the writer, so that eventually the child does this alone. It is what children bring to print that is important, in terms of their use of language; their understanding of formal book language through being read to; and their seach for meaning and order in the way they explore the text with adults or other children. Liz Waterland (1985) calls this 'an apprenticeship approach' and her book *Read with Me* is one of the most impressive practical books I have found on reading which also contains a theoretical base.

Taking account of this background, it is no surprise to suggest that, by the time children reach the stage of 'real' reading and 'real' writing, they are already a considerable way along the route to literacy.

Writing

In order to put the development of writing into context, it is necessary to return to the chapter on Representation. Writing is an aspect of language, but it is also an aspect of representation. Winnicott (1971) proposed the importance of the transitional object in the early development of representation. Baby Lion stood for the link between the mother and the child as well as the space between them when they were apart. Baby Lion was both Ellen's first possession and creation. Vygotsky, in agreement with Winnicott, goes further. He is quite clear that early representation leads directly to written language. He points out that gesture is of paramount importance: playthings and drawings initially acquire meaning supported by gesture. A pencil becomes a person. A book cannot become a person, but its dark green cover could allow it to be turned into a forest. Gradually, objects acquire a meaning independent of gesture. Make-believe, says Vygotsky (1978), is a major contributor to the development of written language. So is drawing.

Representation is one of the keys to writing. Vygotsky's thinking is very much in tune with that of Marie Clay (1975) whose work has been an important influence on research and thinking about early writing. She postulates that children need to construct their own writing system, a theory of their own which they can operate. They need to be allowed to experiment and develop their own theories. This early writing must be unhindered by external demands for neat letter forms, proper spacing, writing on the line, and conventional spelling. Recently, the influence of the work of Emilia Ferreiro and Anna Teberosky (1983) has grown. They feel, like Vygotsky and Marie Clay, that thinking about early writing has overemphasised the graphic shapes (the figurative aspects) and underemphasised the constructive aspects (the rules of composition). Handwriting, letter formation, legibility and speed have tended to be the main focus of adults helping young children to learn to write. Like Vygotsky, Ferreiro and Teberosky believe that children first try to 'find the frontier that differentiates drawing from writing'.

Initially, children begin to put letters into their pictures, but Ferreiro and Teberosky (1983) suggest that the letters do not 'say' anything by themselves.

There is only a vague relationship between letters and drawing. Ferreiro and Teberosky trace the evolution of writing in considerable detail, and while Marie Clay (1975) has identified seven principles, they have established five levels of development in early writing.

During the early stages, children do not use the alphabetic code much, but the first use of it usually occurs through the letters of their own name. Yetta Goodman (1984, p. 106) illuminates this further:

> When told to write his name, three-year-old Josh wrote what appeared to be a small J. As he did this, he said, 'This is a boy.' Then, without further probing, he wrote a much larger character J which resembled the first form and he said, 'This is Dad.' Finally at the bottom of the page, he made the same character even larger, adding a second character which looked like an O superimposed over the first and said, 'This is the boy and Dad together.'

Josh's father's name is Joseph. Although the child was using characters that resembled the first two letters of both his and his father's name, these characters did not represent sounds for him; they represented 'the boy' and 'the Dad'. The child was able to represent his meanings in written language and then meaning signified something in the child's personal experience.

Goodman then goes on to argue that, after children have experimented with size, shape and number to 'invent' written language forms, they begin to develop more conventional alphabetic forms in line with oral and written language (see Figures 6.2, 6.3 and 6.4).

In the following example, six-year-old Raymond uses the R to represent himself, the D to represent his foster mother Daphne, and the H, his foster father Hywel.

Figure 6.1

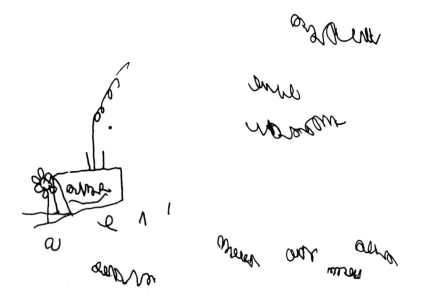

Figure 6.2   David (5 years)

Some letters are easier to write than others. Prospective parents choosing names, please note! Curves, such as those in C and in J with an open semicircle, are difficult.

Ferreiro's work adds support to Marie Clay's. Children do not seem to be 'taught' capital letters by ignorant, tiresome parents, although teachers often accuse innocent parents of this! Children probably use them, if Piaget is right, because they select patterns to draw which they can draw easily. They use complete enclosures and trajectories, separately and in combination. This means that, broadly speaking, they tend to use capitals first, and the more difficult lower case letters later.

The alphabetic symbols occurring in the child's name could well be the stepping-stone towards conventional writing. I remember using a nail file to carve my name with painstaking care in capitals on the wooden mantlepiece. My mother tells me I was four years old.

Like the transitional object, the child's name is both the child's possession and creation. It is not yet conventional writing, but it should be treated with all the respect which the child's possessions demand. Amanda, aged three, is adamant that she does her As on their sides. In other words,

Figure 6.3   Romina (4 years). Writing sample from level 2.

hands off! Like Ellen and Baby Lion, as Winnicott suggests, no one can presume to alter it in any way.

So, for Ferreiro and Teberosky the first stage is drawings and writing mixed (Figure 6.2). When children enter the next stage (Figure 6.3), they may not yet use recognisable

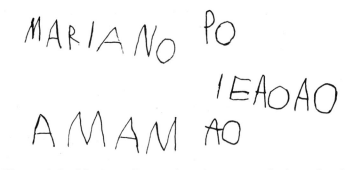

Figure 6.4   Mariano (5 years). Writing sample from level 3 (syllabic).

letters. If they do, these are usually capitals; they vary the type of characters, and the number of characters (anything from three to five), and place them in a line.

During the next stage (Figure 6.4) the children try to let a character stand for a syllable. This is a qualitative leap forward, although there may still be no conventional letter forms. There is now a conflict for children between their syllabic hypothesis and minimum quantity. For example, AMA stands for Amanda, and matches the number of syllables in her name. BO+ stands for Ben, but does not match the number of syllables in his name. The children tend to put in a 'dummy' (extra marks), because of their minimum rule. They must have three 'letters' to make a word.

Again, the child's own name cannot be given too much emphasis. It may be the first 'fixed string', as Ferreiro and Teberosky (1983, p. 207) call it, that the child meaningfully encounters. It serves a useful purpose in causing internal conflict in the child. Striving to resolve this conflict takes the child into the next level. The child needs to find an analysis which goes beyond the syllabic hypothesis. We need to remember that it is the child who constructs this hypothesis. The environment, and the fixed string of the child's name, and the names of significant people, do not always fit in with their hypothesis. It needs modifying. Children constantly vacillate between syllabic and alphabetic.

During the next stage, according to Ferreiro and Terberosky, children have broken the code. This links with Bruner's symbolic mode of representation. The children seem to understand that each written character corresponds happy with different spellings of the same word because 'they mean the same thing', although they are becoming aware that there is a customary way. The child's name is usually the first stable written string.

Children who 'can't even write their own name' on school entry are entering a system which is geared towards level 5 of a long developmental sequence. As Ferreiro asks, should children be placed at an educational disadvantage because they are not at that point on the developmental continuum? This makes life very difficult for a child like Raymond, who is showing healthy, normal writing development, but, for good reasons, at a delayed rate. Ferreiro suggests that children need to go through levels 1–4 before they can tackle the alphabetic code.

She says (Ferreiro and Teberosky, 1983, p. 277), 'Let children write, even in a writing system different from the alphabetic one. We must let them write, not so (that) they invent their own idiosyncratic system, but so (that) they discover that their system is not the conventional one, and in this way find valid reasons to substitute their own hypotheses with our conventional ones.'

It is a serious matter when children enter school at five years old, knowing that they don't know how to write their own names and believing that only by tracing and copying will they come to know. 'The distance between copy writing and children's spontaneous writing is as great as the distance between copy drawing and children's spontaneous drawing (Ferreiro and Teberosky, 1983, p. 278).'

If children entering school are seen as deficient in knowledge of the alphabetic code, and in dire need of swift initiation into it, the teaching of writing will be tackled by asking them to trace letters, copy sentences, correctly form their letters, and as soon as possible introduce punctuation, spelling and grammar.

Lucy Calkins' (1983) work suggests that this is not a particularly efficient method. She observed classrooms in one school in the USA, and became increasingly convinced that there may be better ways of helping children to become writers, and to tackle the mechanics of handwriting, punctuation, grammar and composition. She worked on Donald Graves' (1983) principle that the adult's role is to help children 'find their own voice'. Teachers can, of course, help children to use other people's voices very competently, but if we are talking about educating young children, we want our efforts to lead somewhere useful later on. This means that children need to find and then learn to use their own voice, not someone else's.

Both Ferreiro and Clay suggest that at an early age, in the first five years, children can be truly educated in the writing process. Graves and Calkins believe that this might be continued later on in the educational process. There is a desire in this approach to build on what the child already knows and, with adult help and peer group help, progress from there. The two-year-old who draws and makes believe is perhaps already sharing creations with the significant people in his or her life, and this is the basis of writing.

The child's development in representation (in this case, writing) needs to be linked with the adult's role in helping the child's writing to develop optimally. Vygotsky is helpful here. He says:

> Every function of the child's cultural development appears twice: first on the social level, and later on the individual level; first, between people (interpsychological) and then inside the child (intra-psychological) . . . All the higher functions originate as actual relations between human beings (1978, p. 57).

In the last chapter, representation was seen, in Winnicott's theory, to originate in the interactions between mother and child. Denny Taylor (1983, p. 87) sees the family as the base of literacy: 'Literacy is part of the very fabric of family life.' (We ought perhaps to add 'in some cultures'.)

Denny Taylor also believes that 'literacy can be a barrier between home and school, and a contrivance of familial dissent (1983, p. 87)'. For example, Andrew would not do word and picture matching with his mother. Instead, he made the cards intended for this purpose into an eagle, which he cherished. His mother sensibly gave up!

Some of the children in Taylor's study ran into problems on school entry. She states:

> A skills approach to writing runs counter to the natural development of reading and writing as complex cultural activities (Taylor, 1983, p. 90).

Denny Taylor's naturalistic study is given force through an important long-term study by Berrueta-Clement *et al.*

(1984). This reiterates the harmful effects of an overemphasis on skills work in the early years of education.

The way that the family's approach to literacy meets the school's approach to it is a very important consideration in working with young children, but the way that the child interacts with his or her own family in relation to literacy is also important. Denny Taylor's work supports the view that the personalities involved, the education style of the parents, are dominant factors in shaping the literate experiences of the children within the home. From the beginning the child is both active and reactive to his or her own family's literate experiences and presentations of them. Parents find that each of their children differs in responses to 'writing.' At three years, Hannah would 'write' in zigzagging cursive a shopping list whenever her mother did so. She loved to sign greetings cards with a capital H. She loved stories, often demanding them during the day, as well as expecting as many as possible at bedtime.

At three years, William, from the same family, the second child, would just about concentrate for a bedtime story. Mother had to work hard to keep his concentation, whether he chose stories or whether she did. However, he loved to lie in bed and listen to his five-and-a-half-year-old sister read to him until he fell asleep. This also helped her reading to develop, of course! At four years, William began to enjoy his bedtime story with mother, often choosing the same one several nights in a row for example, *The Tale of Mr Jeremy Fisher* by Beatrix Potter. He would not tolerate any deviation from the text, which he knew inside out. He showed no interest in writing, except for the W of his name with which he would sign the occasional drawing. He was at Ferreiro's stage 2.

At four years, Hannah was reading a few words, such as 'Hannah', 'Mummy' . . . and writing all the time in Ferreiro's stages 3 and 4. By five years, she had 'cracked' the alphabetic code. At four and a half years, William began writing his name frequently, and then cutting it out and sticking it on to models he had made. By five and a half years, he had cracked the alphabetic code, and was always asking his mother for just one more episode of a story. He showed no desire to write, except for his name, but constantly wanted his mother to write notes as reminders to do things.

Denny Taylor's study suggests that teachers also need to be more flexible in the way they meet children's literacy development. Different children are at different points on Ferreiro's continuum, and moreover different personalities go about practising those strategies they possess, and developing new ones, in very different ways.

Shirley Brice Heath (1983), amongst others, has stressed the importance of the teacher tuning into the child's family. What is the family's understanding of and approach to literacy? To bedtime stories? Denny Taylor (1983, p. 54) shows us how families 'salute and hurt' each other through print. For example, seven-year-old Hannah writes her mother a note: 'I'm terribly sorry about the nail varnish remover.' Mother writes to father, 'You are late. Supper burnt. Serves you right.'

Children learn about the multiplicity of literate activities as they learn about different social practices (e.g. birthday cards, shopping lists, bills). Anderson and Stokes (1984) in the USA see writing as an integral part of food-gathering, acquisition and maintenance of shelter and clothing, transportation, entertainment, recreation — that is to say, important in many of the essential areas of human activity.

In fact, children often engage in writing activities of which the parent is unaware. Scraps of paper might exist all over the house, with phone messages, reminders, stories and so on which are purposeful and functional. The home is where children are introduced to functional literacy. Its importance cannot be overemphasised.

There is a potential problem if those working with young children from outside the family setting attempt to tell parents what they should do, whether in the school setting, or the day nursery, or during home visits. This is a partnership on professional terms. An equal partnership demands a more reciprocal approach to the relationship.

In our earlier explorations of representation in this chapter, we looked at the need to give children experiences which build on those of their home life. A child might have been to the corner shop, or the market, or the supermarket. Any of these experiences can be added to or exploited further. Another consideration is the need for children to imitate. Seeing adults involved in functional writing, at the bank, making shopping lists with the children, writing notes for the milkman, is important in this respect. Writing needs to be demonstrated in a functional and purposeful way, so that children can select what they will represent or write about.

A student on teaching practice took in plenty of junk for the three- to four-year-olds in the nursery school. She set it out attractively, made herself very available by sitting at the table, and the children flocked to make models. John experimented with glue, covering the box! Segun had a plan to make a car. No two models were the same, and not all were representational. The student was not imposing her theme of 'shape' on this group of children, although there was plenty of skilful 'shape' talk popped in at appropriate moments, in sensitive ways. Donald Graves might say that the student was helping the children to find their own voice, rather than to echo the thoughts of the adult, which is narrow, and passive, and soon becomes boring. However, if children are to find their own voice they need a great deal of support, help and encouragement from adults, since to do this is much harder than copying. If they are to reach satisfaction and a sense of fulfilment, they need to be helped through the inevitable struggles involved in any worthwhile activity. Being there at the right moment to hold the glue pot still, to stretch out the sticky tape for it to be cut by the child, to hear the story the child has woven around the model, to suggest painting it — all these actions by adults are part of encouraging representation and have implications for early writing. In early writing work, representation is a key factor. It links first feeling encounters with the possible worlds that Margaret Meek stresses.

In attempting to do this it has been necessary to refer back to previous chapters. And it is also necessary to value the family's contribution. Children need a wealth of first-hand experiences to make learning meaningful, and to set it in a functional and purposeful context. Representation is important in all its facets, in stories, dance, songs, home corners, dolls'houses, constructional toys, paints, models, drawings. Amongst all this, children can be encouraged to 'write', in the classroom post office, restaurant, hairdresser, bank and so on. 'Real writing' is only the culmination of a long process towards it. For example, when there is a fight in the home corner, or between two puppets, the children may in fact be looking for a 'lead sentence' as is necessary in the writing process. Early dramatic play helps children to explore roles and themes, beginnings, endings, transitions, all of which are vital to the writing process. When a child does four apparently identical drawings, they may be the equivalent of attempts to revise and redraft in the writing process. Two children, William and Tom, discuss a drawing. Both are four years old. 'Why is its mouth there?' 'It's hungry, silly. That's its tongue, going like that.' He sticks out his tongue. They break into laughter.

Frank Smith (1983) believes that at first representational work is the child's creation, to be admired, but not submitted like a manuscript to be scrutinised and criticised. He is in agreement with Winnicott in this. The creation belongs to the child. No one else can presume to alter it in any way. Vygotsky says that the willingness to take criticism, to submit a manuscript for the scrutiny of others, emerges from the social relationship formed with the 'interested person', who is invited by the child to share in and work on the creation.

Just as there needs to be a truly reciprocal relationship between parents and professionals, so there needs to be a reciprocal relationship between child and adults who will manage to extend development in an educative way. Joan Tamburrini (1982) sees this informal teaching as the strength of nursery education. Teaching does not have to be direct and formal to be 'teaching'.

Conclusion

In this chapter, we have discovered that the principles of self-activity and self-regulation stand firm, that the whole child is important, that freedom to learn is necessary. We have seen that we cannot compartmentalise areas of development or knowledge. Early writing is bound up with representation, which is part of total development. In recent years, our knowledge of early writing has progressed, as we have seen in this exploration of the writing process. There is a clear difference between the processes and the products of human development. Representation as an aspect of processes and products bears this out. Adults working with young children need to bear in mind that processes determine products. A thought from Aesop draws together this chapter: 'Beware you do not lose the substance through grasping at the shadow.'

7 Significant Other People for the Child

There is a range of people who are significant in one way or another to the development of a young child. In particular, family, professional workers and other children whom the child meets regularly all become important for that child in a direct way.

In this chapter, the impact of the family, professional workers and other children is discussed in turn, with particular reference to the role of the early childhood educator.

Family

It is no longer appropriate to write of 'family' in the sense of two parents and their children, with father working and mother at home, or working part-time. As Gillian Pugh and Erica De'Ath (1984, p. 23) point out, the family is 'simply what you find behind the door, and variation, whether by chance or choice, is now the norm'. People who work with young children need to adjust to this situation. There is a tendency for professionals to be judgemental about the child's family, because they focus on the child rather than the child in context. This often leads to professionals undermining the parents' confidence in their ability to be good parents. Ignoring the child's home, and the people in it, means that the child is denied the opportunity for continuity between home and school. We demand that the child lives in two worlds, and ignore the fact that, of the two, the home is the more influential and lasting influence, unless the two work together. As Gillian Pugh and Erica De'Ath state:

> The great majority of parents are concerned to do their best for their children, even if they are not always sure what this might be (1984, p. 169).

Every family is different, and has different needs. The key to partnership with parents lies in having a network of strategies which can be employed so that different approaches are used with different families, approaches which support and build on the families rather than undermining what the parents do. Some families do not wish to or cannot come into school often. Some families enjoy being in school, but in the parents' room, not the classroom. Others prefer to be visited at home. Others want workshops, meetings, films, talks in the evenings or at weekends after school, often provided that there is a crèche. Others will make equipment, raise funds, come to social functions, but do not want further contact. Some parents actively seek help in child-rearing and in the education of their children, others do not.

The teacher's role is to build a partnership with every parent. Clearly, it is easier to do this with some parents than with others. Situations involving suspected child abuse, whether physical, mental, or sexual, are the most difficult, and where this exists, the teacher needs to work with other professionals as much as with the parents. However, the tendency of professionals to undermine any parent's self-confidence with their 'expertise', and the isolation felt by many bringing up young children, were seen to be contributing to the difficulties experienced by many parents (Pugh and De'Ath, 1984, p. 197).

Most parents are not interested in children *in general*. Their main concern is with their own child and the child's friends. They are not teachers, nor do they wish to be. Teachers and parents do not bring the same qualities to the partnership. Their roles are complementary, and should not be seen as threatening to each other. The parent is highly emotionally linked to the child, and prepared to go to 'unreasonable lengths' for the child as Elizabeth Newson's study (1972; quoted in Kellmer Pringle, 1980, p. 37) shows. Alice Honig (1984) stresses the need for parents and professionals to build specific observations together. Professionals can help parents to look in more detail at what their child can do, and this helps both teacher and parents to work together for the child. In this way, the teacher can help the parents to use the power and energy of their feelings for their child, and can build and extend on the parents' work through his or her knowledge of children in general.

Parents want their children to be happy in school. So do teachers. Parents want their children to be successful at reading, writing, mathematics, and to be well-behaved and popular. So do teachers. The aims of parents and teachers in fact coincide in important areas. Teachers who look below the surface of what parents are saying can find a shared basis for work on which trust can be built. But teachers need to share what they know about child development, curriculum, provision, and not to guard it.'

Chris Athey (1980, p. 7) postulates a typology of parental involvement which can be added to (as indicated below by Bruce).

Type 1
Parents recognising or trying to extend the learning of their child (Athey).

Type 2
Parents who are eager to work with teachers in the classroom in ways which do not fit in with the teachers' methods (Bruce).

Type 3
Parents bodily in school, but not active in the classroom (Athey).

Type 4
Parents whose main contact with the school is bringing and fetching children, and perhaps attending parents' evenings (Bruce).

Type 5
Parents who do not bring children to school, or seek contact with school (Athey).

The following examples show how a teacher can work with a wide variety of parents as described above.

Type 1 *Parents recognising or trying to extend the learning of the child*

Three-year-old Shanaz's father was a bus driver. He wanted to be with his children as much as possible, and managed to arrange his shift work accordingly. He brought Shanaz to nursery school whenever he could and normally stayed for half an hour. (He brought his younger child, a toddler, with him, too.) He wanted to know what was the purpose of each activity. He took great pleasure in watching Shanaz in the nursery once he realised that water play and other messy activities could be used to teach her mathematical language, — for example, 'out of the water', 'in the water', 'high', 'low', 'long way' and so on. He used these terms with relish as she played. He was 'teaching' his daughter mathematics. His enthusiasm was invigorating for the staff, who found him a positive adult to welcome into the school. His basic trust of the teacher's knowledge made it easier for the school staff to work with him.

Type 2 Parents who are eager to work with teachers in ways which do not fit in with the teachers' methods

It is not for teachers to tell families how to bring up their children, or to insist that education must be approached in one way — the school's way. Just as teachers need to establish a child's intentions and build on them in educationally worthwhile ways, so they need to find out what parents think education is, and what they think teachers are for, before they can begin a successful partnership. All too often the parents are asked to listen to the teacher's view of education, but not the reverse. Parents need to know what teachers are trying to do, but teachers need to know what parents consider to be important. This is the basis of mutual respect — respect for each other's expertise, respect for each other's commitment to a particular child, respect for the different skills and strengths each brings to a complementary partnership. Two examples follow which show how the teacher can use his/her skills to encourage appropriate parental involvement.

Five-year-old Betty's mother liked to work in the classroom. She was eager to 'teach' an activity. The teacher suggested that she helped the children to make dough and use it. She wanted Betty's mother to see her do this activity with the children before she had a group on her own. Betty's mother couldn't resist joining in while the teacher worked with the group. The teacher asked an open-ended question: 'I wonder what we do first?' Betty's mother instantly swooped in: 'We need a bowl, spoon, flour . . .' She began transmitting the knowledge. This was how she saw the role of the teacher, not asking obtuse questions that didn't get to the point. The teacher suggested that Betty's mother should all the time check what children learned by asking them questions about what they were doing. Betty's mother accepted and acted on this, as it was part of her view of education — teach the knowledge, then test the knowledge. Over a period of a year Betty's mother and the teacher began to discuss the importance of getting children to anticipate what will happen, to plan what will happen, to organise equipment they will need. Initially, the teacher built on the parent's view of a teacher's role and so did not undermine her confidence and did not reject her views.

Some parents experience difficulty in leaving their child in school. They are sometimes unfairly referred to as clinging or over-protective. They are often parents who enjoy a very close relationship with their children, and are very sensitive to their child's feelings and deeply concerned about their child's education.

When five-year-old Stephanie made a preliminary visit to the reception class, prior to beginning school, her mother instantly settled down to work with her and the group of children at the construction toy table. She talked to each child about what he or she was doing, and skilfully involved Stephanie in contributing, and in talking to the child next to her. So far, so good. When Stephanie began to attend regularly at school, her mother wanted to stay until she was 'settled'. The teacher suggested, on the second day, that her mother should take a short coffee break in the staffroom. Stephanie cried. Mother would not leave her. Next day, Stephanie began to cling to her mother all the time, anticipating that she would try to have coffee. Mother reassured her, insisting that she would not leave her at all. Stephanie wanted her mother very close to her, and stopped attempting to relate to the other children. By the end of the week, the pattern was set. Stephanie would not become involved in activities. Neither could her mother become involved, because Stephanie thwarted any attempt she made to work with groups of children. Stephanie's mother was upset. She felt that she had done all the 'right things', and yet her child would not let her go at all. Her 'good' mothering was being punished instead of rewarded. She needed the teacher as someone to help her who was not involved in this 'eyeball-to-eyeball' situation. The teacher could not discuss anything with the mother since Stephanie clung to her, so she asked her to phone from home. The teacher then discussed strategies, telling her that this was a not uncommon experience for very good, sensitive, devoted parents. Of course, Stephanie did not want such a treasured person to leave. She suggested that Stephanie's mother and school should take a united approach, and insist that she left for 15 minutes immediately on school arrival, warning Stephanie that this would happen. In this way, Stephanie did not have the worry of anticipating her mother's going until coffee time. They would gradually increase the time in discussion together. Once Stephanie was settled, her mother would be able to come into school and work with the children, say once a week, since she wanted to be involved in the classroom. At this stage, it would be too complicated for Stephanie to grasp that pattern. They needed to wait until she was established. In this way, the teacher reassured the mother that she could be trusted with her child, and would be sensitive towards her. She made it clear that she thought highly of her parenting, understood her child's behaviour and wanted to welcome her to the classroom in principle, but the timing of this had to revolve around what would be appropriate for Stephanie. Stephanie's mother relaxed. So did Stephanie, who settled into school happily during that term. The next term, her mother came regularly to school to help with cooking, reading, model-making and so on.

Type 3 *Parents bodily in school, but not active in the classroom.*

Some parents, if encouraged, will often linger in or near the classroom after having brought their child to school. They will also come in on other occasions, but will resist greater involvement. The teacher or nursery nurse needs to develop strategies for encouraging the parents' interest in their children into active expression. Three-year-old Khaliq's mother regularly brought him to school, and went immediately to the book corner, where she was friendly, but did not seek contact with the teacher while her child settled into school. Here, a different strategy was needed. Khaliq's mother was in school regularly, but as yet there was no partnership with the teacher. Each week, there was cookery, and the teacher asked her if she would make chapatis with the children. She said her English was not good enough, but the teacher encouraged her to speak in Urdu. She enjoyed the cookery session, and stayed on for the end-of-the-morning singing, sitting with the teacher and children. She liked the songs, which included 'Humpty Dumpty'. The teacher explained that the song was to help the children use mathematical language ('up' and 'down'), and that tomorrow she would do 'The Grand Old Duke of York'. She invited the mother to join the session. Mother was delighted, and was heard saying 'up' and 'down' to Khaliq as they went out. The next step was to encourage the mother to watch her child with the teacher. Khaliq was observed putting a pile of bricks into the classroom 'telephone kiosk' one by one — and then, once a pile had formed, picking each one up and throwing it into a large cardboard box outside the kiosk. He did this for some time. He was transporting, and placing objects in containers. The teacher asked if he did anything like this at home. He had put a pile of dried chick-peas into a saucepan from a colander, but his mother could not explain this in English. She demonstrated with equipment in the home corner, and the following day brought in chick-peas and demonstrated again. Meanwhile, the teacher had organised a paint-mixing activity with Khaliq in mind. This involved putting powder paint into pots and adding water. Khaliq did this for half an hour. His mother was beginning to see how reporting his home activities to the teacher was important, as the teacher used this information in her lesson planning. She began to see that activities were planned, and that mess was necessary and could lead to science. The 'mixtures' were an early chemistry lesson, the teacher explained. So was the cookery lesson, making chapatis — these were both examples of changing a substance: from powder (paint) to sludgy liquid (paint and water) and from powdery flour to a solid chapati. This activity is a precursor to understanding chemical equations. Khaliq's mother could see that the teacher wanted him to learn mathematics (up and down songs). She gradually became more relaxed about messy activities because she could see that they led on to science and maths.

This example also demonstrates the indirect approach to structuring the curriculum in the interactionist style. One of the central aims of this approach is to respect the parent's view, and not to demand assimilation of these views into the school's model. The problem with formally structured approaches is that parents have to be initiated into the school's view of education, and inducted into a particular 'method'. This is one of the criticisms made of the High/Scope programme pioneered by David Weikert (Sylva *et al.*, 1986). In contrast, the indirectly-structured curriculum more easily allows for integration of the parents' view with the school's view. Parents are not required to lay

aside their own ideas, but to broaden them. The same applies to the teachers, who are also required to keep up to
date through in-service training as part of being articulate in
the broadening process. Broadening thinking does not mean
watering it down. It means parents and teachers clarifying
their own ideas through meeting other ideas. This is not an
easy, or comfortable, way for teachers to work, but it is a
deeply satisfying and successful way to involve parents, as
the work of Lin Poulton (1979) in Hampshire and Chris
Athey (1972–6) in London suggests.

Betty's mother and Khaliq's parents were asked to
broaden their views, but not to abandon them. The teacher
reached out to touch on areas of overlap in their view of
school and home, and to build from there. In the next section, the same approach was applied to Kim's mother.

Barbara Tizard *et al.* (1981) make the point that Asian
parents are difficult to involve in the curriculum because
teachers do not make them aware of the importance of
messy activities or play. Teachers need to demonstrate the
importance of these to every parent. Valuing messy home
activities (cookery) and giving them high status in school,
is one starting point. Khaliq's mother also liked gardening,
and grew vegetables in school, as she lived in a flat with no
garden. Outdoor activities were then given high value. This
is another area which is often not seen to be important by
parents. Studying worms, snails, slugs and the different
properties of soils (clay, sand, and gravel) is messy, but leads
to natural science. By beginning with what the parent
valued, cooking and gardening, the teacher was able to share
the importance of messy and outdoor activities with this
parent, over a period of time. Khaliq's mother also began,
very gradually, to see the need to observe the child before
planning lessons, so that the lesson was effective and appropriate, and to see that her observations mattered as well
as the teacher's. She became active in the classroom, cooking, gardening, helping with paintings and so on, using her
strengths. She was a home garment-maker, and a sewing
machine was set up for her in the classroom where she
made clothes for the dressing-up corner, or for her child, out
of a big box of materials which was always available — and
she let the children have turns, too.

She did not see herself as a teacher. Her presence enriched
the classroom activities, introduced Urdu alongside

English, and helped the teacher through her developing skill in observing her own child. Her interest was in her child. In doing the activities she enjoyed, in which the children participated, she enhanced rather than threatened the teacher's role. Khaliq's father visited the school to 'inspect it' when Khaliq first came. The teacher talked about the curriculum, mainly the beginnings of the three Rs. Khaliq's father came when dolls' wash day was in progress. He was about to leave this 'women's activity' and take his son to something else. The teacher told him that this was a mathematics lesson. She explained to him that she and his wife had noted Khaliq transporting objects and putting them into containers. This washing activity had been designed to help Khaliq to do both. It helped his ability to make a series (largest, smallest clothes to peg out) it helped him to classify (soapy water, rinsing water and so on). She explained that Khaliq needed to both seriate and classify in order to be ready for number work later on. She demonstrated this difficult theory in a practical context. Father and son stayed at the activity. Khaliq's father did not visit again, but gave his approval for his wife to continue bringing Khaliq (for nursery education is non-statutory).

The developing partnership in Khaliq's family took a year to become established, and a further year to flourish. Most teachers only work with a group of children for one year and so the importance of working with colleagues as a team, and of a whole school policy in relation to work with parents, requires emphasis. The importance of five terms in the nursery where the partnership pattern is established also requires consideration.

Type 4 *Parents whose main contact with the school is bringing and fetching children, and attending parents' evening*

Five-year-old Kim's mother brought and fetched her each day, would have a quick chat with the teacher, but had shown no sign of wishing to become involved in the classroom. She was anxious for Kim to learn to read and write. As is quite common, she saw teaching Kim to do this as the main function of school. She had taught Kim to write her name before she came to school. There was a problem here in that the mother was also encouraging Kim to copy words. This differed from the school's approach, which advocated developmental writing where children are encouraged initially to 'invent' spellings rather than copy, and where children are introduced to conventional spelling gradually. Here was a clash between home and school. Kim's mother was not going to be convinced that the way she herself learned to write 'was wrong', because she successfully learned to write that way. Ideally, the mother would already have been made aware of the school's approach in the nursery, but there was no nursery education in the area. The teacher organised an exhibition of written work from reception to top infants, asking her colleagues to help her. As parents brought their children in or collected them, she referred to this. She showed Kim's mother what the school did. Kim's mother was reassured to see the high standard of spelling and large amounts of writing many children achieved later in the school. She was interested to see that some writing was stories, even poems, some children wrote about outings or events, some annotated models they had made, or experiments they had performed. She was introduced to different modes of writing. Her concept of 'writing' broadened, but the teacher did not undermine her. She congratulated the mother on teaching Kim the alphabet and especially on starting with the letters of her name. She was pleased that she had taught Kim to be enthusiastic about writing and feel that she could write. She asked her to write down stories Kim wanted to tell, so that she (as teacher) could make them into a book for Kim. As Kim was not used to 'inventing' spelling with her mother, the teacher worked on this aspect with her in school. In this way, she protected the child/parent relationship from possible failure during what might have been a difficult transition. Once Kim became confident in her own ability to 'have a go' at spelling, she began spontaneously to do this with her mother. Her mother did not automatically 'correct' the spelling. She left it unless it was one of the spellings she and the teacher had decided to work on (e.g. 'wood' for 'would'). The teacher said, when Kim's mother met her from school, that she wanted to work on the 'ould' family of words, since Kim consistently spelt this sound 'oo'.

Home and school were working together successfully. Kim's mother had not been asked to abandon her views of how children learn to write. She had broadened it, which had been an exciting rather than an undermining experience. In this partnership, it was the ten minutes before and after school which were of critical importance. Kim's mother also attended any evening 'talks' to parents about different aspects of the curriculum.

Gillian Pugh and Erica De'Ath (1984) point out that listening to and acting on parent's views of education does not mean that parents take over the teacher's role. It seems to enhance the teacher's work. Pugh and De'Ath (1984, p. 178) refer to McGeeney:

> Approaches which involve parents in reading and mathematics workshops where they can work through problems as their children have, and where there is a relaxed atmosphere for discussing all aspects of schooling, have an important part to play if parents are to increase their understanding and their confidence in involvement (McGeeney, 1980).

Type 5 *Parents who do not bring children to school, or seek contact with school*

Behaviour of this sort is unusual and ought to be an instant signal for the teacher to attempt to make contact with the parents, in a sensitive way. The problem is how. Three-year-old Jerome's parents are an example of this type. They did not attempt any contact with the school until the teacher sought it. Indeed, they seemed quite antipathetic and involvement with them required intermediary help from the health visitor. This example is discussed in full in the next section (on professional workers) because, as in many instances of complete lack of contact with parents, the support of other professional workers was necessary.

In this section on families, a network of strategies that teachers can use has been discusssed. Different families have different needs. Having a variety of approaches helps the parent/teacher partnership to develop with success, which means that significant people in the child's life are working together for the child.

In the next section, on professionals in statutory and voluntary agencies, the need for the teacher to work with a variety of adults as well as parents is emphasised. Being child-centred is too narrow an approach. It is more appropriate to consider the child-in-context, and that includes the different skills and strengths that different professionals and voluntary agencies have to offer in strengthening the child, as a member of a family (Bartholomew, 1985).

Professionals in statutory and voluntary agencies

There are two facts which need to be borne in mind in thinking about this group of significant adults. First, the range and types of educational and related provision are varied, and this can have a significant impact on the types of professionals involved with the child. For the under-fives the variety is bewildering and difficult to justify. Even for the five- to seven-year-olds (i.e. after the statutory school age), the variety is wide. A considerable proportion of children under the age of five attend playgroups affiliated to the Pre-School Playgroups Association which is a voluntary agency. In many parts of the country children attend nursery classes in primary or nursery schools run by local education authorities (LEAs). Some children attend private nursery schools or day nurseries. A very few children attend family centres or combined centres jointly funded by both LEAs and social services departments. Other children are placed with child-minders, both registered and unregistered. Hughes *et al.* (1980) point out that there is considerable variety of provision according to the geographical area.

Even at five years of age there is no uniformity of provision. There are separate infant schools, infant classes in primary schools, and infant classes in first schools.

Secondly, it is important to bear in mind that, according to the Warnock Report (DES, 1978), one in six children in Great Britain at any time, and one in five at some stage in their school lives, will have a special need and this means that the stereotype of the teacher being the only significant professional involved with the child is misleading. In other words, a considerable proportion of children will require a fairly wide range of multi-professional help which goes beyond the teacher, play leader, nursery nurse or even the health visitor and general practitioner (GP). These other professionals will include the social worker (generic or specialist), educational psychologist, child psychiatrist, play therapist, speech therapist and so on.

The 1981 Education Act states: 'A child has a special need if he/she has learning difficulty significantly greater than the majority of children of that age, or a disability which prevents the use of educational facilities of a kind generally provided in the schools for children of that age.' If this special need reaches a significant level, a 'statement' of the child's needs must be prepared which should involve all the professionals working with the child and the parents. However, this is not to imply that only children with special needs require multi-professional help. Every child needs this, though perhaps not such a wide range of support from professionals and voluntary agencies.

These two points, varied provision and special needs, illustrate that a range of professionals and agencies may become involved significantly in a child's life. However, the professionals most likely to impinge on the child's life are GPs, health visitors, playgroup leaders, nursery nurses and teachers. Other children meet social workers, educational psychologists and specialists of different kinds. In the remainder of this section a number of examples are given which show interactions between parents and professionals and among professionals, and conclusions are drawn as to good and bad practice.

Jane

In the early stages of the child's life, the GP and health visitor are likely to be the key professionals. Health visitors can act as catalysts for family development in co-ordination with other professionals. One-year-old Jane's family disliked professional workers as they had had a number of unfortunate experiences over the years. The health visitor found it difficult to gain entrance to their flat and yet she and the GP were concerned about Jane's physical growth and weight. She was small for her age, and not eating well. She was too young to attend a playgroup, and there was no parent/toddler group within easy walking distance. Another of the health visitor's clients had been a nursery teacher until she gave up work to have her child, now a year old, and this mother ran a very small parent/toddler group which met three mornings a week. The health visitor put the two mothers in touch. Because the ex-nursery teacher was 'just another mother' with a one-year-old, she was able to work well with the family. Jane and her mother joined the group of four mothers and four children. Relationships with the health visitor improved. She was seen as someone who could help, but not interfere. Visits to a specialist doctor were positive. The father attended the group when his shift work allowed. They all went to a swimming club together, and had joint outings and celebrated birthdays together, as well as undertaking joint jam-making and bread-making as part of the parent/toddler group activities. The health visitor was asked to provide information regularly. She organised visits from experts on preventive dentistry, family planning and nutrition, and gave information about different nursery provision in the area. At three years old Jane attended a larger playgroup so that her mother could work in the mornings. At four years she attended the nursery class of the local school. The health visitor put the playgroup leader in touch with the parent/toddler group leader when a problem arose over Jane's eating. This was quickly resolved.

In this example, the health visitor had co-ordinated and used the different local resources and called upon specialist medical advice in her attempt to help Jane's family. She was sufficiently skilled to use a volunteer worker's skills when her 'professionalism' was acting as a block in the early stages of her relationship with the family. She valued what other workers could offer at every stage.

In Jane's case, it was the statutory services which 'led', with the health visitor as the key worker, co-ordinating GP, volunteer worker, playgroup and teacher, and specialist medical help. In the following example, the health visitor again 'led'.

Petra

Petra was born blind. She lived in an area where there was no special education support. Her parents were helped initially by the GP and health visitor, who put her in touch with an educational home visitor from a voluntary agency for the blind (Royal National Institute for the Blind). This professional worker helped the family through the first five years of Petra's life, and co-ordinated resources and professional help to such an extent that Petra was able to attend the local primary school. Her role was also to offer emotional support to the family, and to act as a bridge between teachers in the school and the family when problems arose,

which they did frequently. There was a gap in statutory services for this family — no advice on how to stimulate
and manage Petra in the first five years, and no school for
visually impaired children at statutory school age. The LEA
bought special school places from the neighbouring authority. The parents wanted Petra to attend school more locally
and to have friends in the community if possible. The educational home visitor marshalled resources for the family
with specialist equipment and advice on working with
Petra in the earliest years. She supported them in the educational decisions they made and bridged the gap between
home and school. She was a highly-trained paid worker,
employed by a voluntary agency, who had more impact on
this family's life in the first five years of Petra's life than
any statutory worker because of her skill in co-ordinating
the medical and educational resources available. In the example of Jerome which follows, the specialist nursery
teacher was the key worker.

Jerome

Three-year-old Jerome's parents did not come to school. On
his first day at school he was sent on the school bus alone
under the care of the bus supervisor and driver. He was
'deaf', but his hearing aid was in his satchel. It would be
easy for the teacher to draw the conclusion that here was an
uncaring family, insensitive to their child's needs. The
teacher in this special school used a home/school book
with each family since children were spread over a large
catchment area and brought to school by bus. She immediately, on that first day, sent a book home in Jerome's
satchel, asking if she could introduce herself to the parents,
and wondering if they might like to visit the school. The
next day, the book had not been written in. The teacher
could not phone the family as there was no phone, so she
phoned the GP. He was wary of divulging any information
at all — but grudgingly gave the name of the health visitor
for the family. Contact with the health visitor revealed that
both parents worked, and were bewildered by their son
Jerome, who had seemed to hear and had begun to talk at
tow years. He had recently been sent to Jamaica to stay with
his grandmother for six months — and had stopped talking.
On returning home he had been tested and found to have a
hearing loss. The health visitor agreed to find out if the

family would like the teacher to visit. Two days later there was a note in the home book suggesting the teacher might like to call one day after school. The health visitor had found that the parents never looked in the satchel, so were unaware of the existence of the home book.

The teacher set off on the school bus with Jerome on the suggested day and, at the set-down point, found herself to her surprise at Jerome's child-minder's flat. He was picked up from there at 5.30 p.m. (It was now 4.30 p.m.) The child-minder was obviously embarrassed about this, and so the teacher said that she had some shopping to do and would go straight to Jerome's flat later, which she did. When she met the parents at 6.00 p.m., a situation potentially damaging to the parent/teacher partnership had arisen. The parents were clearly embarrassed. To them 'after school' meant after work. They had not wanted the teacher to know that Jerome went to a child-minder. They clearly thought that a teacher would disapprove of this. If an atmosphere of trust and mutual respect was to develop, the teacher's training needed to be used. She had received considerable help in working with parents during her specialist training in working with hearing-impaired children. Over tea, she established an atmosphere whereby she made it clear that she was actively seeking the parents' views, and needed their help in order to do her job. The focus was on everyone working for Jerome. The parents admitted their anger that he had been sent to a special school and their perplexity that he had suddenly stopped talking. They talked about their dislike of the hearing aid which labelled him. They did not want to come to school: they thought they would be upset to see other deaf children. Education to them meant learning to read, beginning with the alphabet, and they supposed that as Jerome was deaf there was no sense in trying to teach him. They just wanted him to be as happy as possible considering he was handicapped. During the visit the teacher *listened* rather than talked. She also conveyed her delight in teaching Jerome — she wanted them to see that she valued their child.

Kaplan (1978; quoted in Honig, 1984, p. 65) talks about the awakening of the unloved self in the parent in the case of a handicapped child. This may well also apply to the parents' relationship with a child at the toddler stage of temper tantrums. When parents ask, 'Has she been good?', they are perhaps really asking, 'Do you like my child?' Jerome was pleased to see his teacher, but she made sure that she emphasised how relaxed and purposeful he was at home, what appropriate toys for his age he had, how she worried because he was always so beautifully turned out and his clothes might get spoiled at school. By the end of the visit, the parents knew that the teacher sympathised with their work pattern and understood the need for a child-minder, and that she obviously liked their son and was committed to working with him. They could trust her to be kind to him. She believed he was learning and she thought them caring parents who fed and clothed their child well and stimulated his development with toys. They invited her to visit again.

The partnership developed positively, through home visits. The teacher contacted the Ear, Nose and Throat specialist, who was very helpful in getting a different hearing aid with automatic volume control. Jerome began to wear it in school. Then the mother took a day off work to come to a coffee morning/talk that the teacher had asked the school's educational psychologist to give. She met other parents and enjoyed it, finding they had similar experiences and difficulties. At the next home visit, the teacher suggested to Jerome's mother that she might like to visit the classroom in action with one of the mothers she had particularly liked. In school the mother was struck by Jerome's speech when he was wearing his hearing aid. She watched the teacher working with the children, and took comfort that Jerome was showing off and in the fact that her new friend's child was, too. All the adults laughed about it and the atmosphere was relaxed.

Gradually the home visits became more focused on Jerome's learning, the curriculum, and care of the hearing aid. Ideas for follow-up activities at home were given. The parents told the teacher what they observed Jerome doing and the teacher shared what happened in school. The parents began to write in the home book. At six years Jerome was beginning to read, talk and lip-read well and was a more relaxed child. He transferred to a partial hearing unit and a year later was integrated successfully into his local primary school, where his parents were able to give him the necessary support. They trusted his teachers, respecting their knowledge, felt able to ask for help and information, felt included in his education, knew they were important, and that the professionals regarded them as good, loving parents.

The key factors in this successful parent/teacher partnership were that the teacher built up the parents' self-confidence and extended what the parents thought education was about rather than displacing their view with something totally different. The teacher marshalled resources and information through a multi-professional approach, working with the health visitor, specialist doctor and educational psychologist. Not all professionals welcomed this contact (in this instance, the GP did not), but the teacher kept going until she found those who also valued a multi-professional approach. She put the parents in touch with other parents to form a self-help group, and used an away-from-school setting prior to encouraging the parents in school.

Where there is little or no contact between professional workers, parents can be left confused, bewildered and let down.

John

Two-year-old John's mother cared deeply about his healthy development. He attended a dentist as soon as his teeth came through. The dentist assured her that his thumb-sucking was not a problem. His mouth would need orthodontic treatment at nine or 10 years anyway, and he was likely to grow out of it by five or six years. Mother relaxed. When John started at nursery school, the nursery nurse discouraged him from sucking his thumb during story time. Mother began to worry again when John reported this. She did not like to mention it to the nursery nurse, who obviously knew more than she did (in her view). At six years of age, John was still sucking his thumb. At eight, the dentist suggested a visit to the orthodontist in preparation for later treatment. She insisted that the thumb-sucking was no problem. The orthodontist greeted John with, 'And what do you do that you shouldn't do?', and was unpleasant to him about it, saying she would do nothing for him until he gave it up. John's mother ventured to say that she had thought treatment would not begin until 10 and that John now only sucked his thumb on going to sleep, or if distressed. The orthodontist gave a smile, but no information. At the next visit to the dentist, the mother reported this back. The dentist closed professional ranks with the orthodontist, and said, 'Well, he's nearly stopped now, hasn't he?' John's mother felt confused about the conflicting professional views displayed in educational and medical contexts. She worried that as a parent she had failed to do right by John, but felt frustrated and angry because she had tried her best.

Cathy

Four-year-old Cathy's family were visited by a number of professional workers. Her 14-year-old uncle was under the supervision of a probation officer. The whole family was visited by a social worker and the health visitor called very regularly. The nursery teacher visited Cathy and her mother once each term as part of the school's home visiting policy. The teacher and probation officer arranged for 14-year-old Paul to come into school and work with his niece, Cathy. This brought out skills he could not use elsewhere — gentleness, patience and so on. Officially, he was mending electrical equipment, which meant that he could hold his head high among his peers. The teacher, social worker and health visitor worked together on financial benefits, nutrition, and stimulating Cathy and her younger sister Sharon. Obviously areas of confidentiality had to be respected, but within that proper constraint the professional workers found that they could ask each other for co-operation and support because of the 'willingness of spirit' and basic trust which had developed between them.

The teacher–nursery nurse professional relationship

The foregoing examples emphasise the variety of professional partnerships which can be significant in the development of a young child. However, the most common partnership, especially within the school, is likely to be that of teacher and nursery nurse. It is one of the most important professional partnerships that can exist. It is worth noting that nursery nurses also work in day nurseries, hospitals and other services dealing with health and social services. They are highly skilled in their knowledge of the whole of the first seven years of the child's life, and in their training pay more attention to the under threes and health and care aspects than does the teacher, as well as studying the child's educational development. The training of the teacher emphasises education, albeit of the whole child (not just the child's thinking) and concentrates on the three to eight years period. When the partnership is strong, the roles of the nursery nurse and the teacher complement each other.

In this book examples of the work of nursery nurses are given which highlight this often powerful partnership. There are times when the teacher leads, and times when the nursery nurse leads. That is the essence of a partnership. One of the difficulties of multi-professional work is that it is often unclear who the acknowledged 'leader' is at a particular time. Some professionals take on the role of leader all the time as if it is their right. GPs and educational psychologists are often accused of this by teachers, health visitors and social workers. Nursery nurses often accuse teachers of this same attitude. The way each profession sees itself is linked with its status, which is linked with how it is regarded by the society in which it functions. A sense of being superior (or subservient) makes a bad starting point for multi-professional work. Both attitudes lose sight of the real work, which is to promote the development of the child in context. If one member of a partnership dominates, it will not be much of a partnership.

Clift *et al.* (1980) talk about the need for different early childhood workers to be clear about their roles, what is expected of them, what their contributions should be. Because the early childhood educator and the nursery nurse literally work in the same room, this becomes particularly important.

A new teacher came to work in a nursery school. The nursery nurse knew all the families, the school routines and how the team operated in the school. She helped the new teacher by reminding her about story times, that each child must be welcomed by the teacher each morning, that reminders of medical examinations must go out. She took responsibility for new children and took the teacher on a home visit so as to introduce her to a family where the mother had just returned home with the new-born baby and so had not yet met the new teacher in school. She made sure that children with allergies had the right food, and that a child with eczema did not play with soap at the water tray, while the teacher got to know the class. She also organised the main activities until the new teacher was able to share and contribute more fully.

In this school the teachers and nursery nurses would meet at the end of the day to check that they had tidied up properly and together jot down observations they had made of children on cards they kept for that purpose. They would plan for the next day, each saying what she wanted to do and why. They would help each other with practical suggestions, especially in relation to their long-term plans. The teachers tended to lead in drawing up these plans formally after they had been discussed and agreed. The teachers kept official records and co-ordinated the curriculum. The nursery nurses made observations both broad and deep through their knowledge of the different facets of child development which enhanced the teachers' view of each child and family and helped them both to plan activities relating to the different curriculum areas of knowledge.

In a partnership it should not be possible to say who is the stronger. Both partners need each other — and both are useful for different purposes. If the teacher simply absorbs the nursery nurse's contribution into her own, the situation is too much dominated by the teacher. If the nursery nurse absorbs the teacher's views into her own, the situation is too much dominated by the nursery nurse. Both approaches to the child are valid and of use in different ways. They are separate, but overlap. They need to be integrated so that each participant is aware of and proud of her particular, different and distinct contribution to the development of the child. In this school the partnership between nursery nurses and teachers had developed into one of mutual respect, resulting in a strong team.

So far in this chapter, significant others in the child's life have been the immediate family and friends, and the professional workers in statutory and voluntary agencies with whom the family has contact. In the next section, relationships with peers are explored. Relating to other children is a theme which pervades this book, and many examples relevant to the section which follows can be found in chapters 5 and 8, under the titles Representation and The Ability to Decentre.

Other children

Adults are not the only significant others for children. Children are also of great importance, both younger and older, both within and beyond the family setting.

Siblings

Judy Dunn (1984) writes about the different chemistry of relationships in different families between brothers and sisters.

Five-year-old Ella and seven-year-old Tom were spending a day with friends. They were introduced to a visitor to the house. 'This is Tom, and this is Ella.' Tom quickly said, 'She's my sister.' He was protecting his sister from being made to speak to someone she did not know. He knew the things that tended to worry him, and applied them to his sister. This brother and sister were very close. Being close does not mean no quarrels. In fact, quarrelling is an important part of developing relationships with other children. In the early stages children tend to hit each other. This is typical of two-year-olds.

Two-year-old Hilary wanted a toy car from her three-year-old brother Joseph. She snatched it, and hit him with the car when he tried to grab it back. The situation was not left here. The father took the car back and gave it to Joseph explaining that she must not grab and hit. Hilary had a temper tantrum. Joseph felt sorry for her — he gave her the car. Father praised Joseph's kindness, and reasserted that Hilary must not hit and grab, but 'ask nicely' for the car next time, and that she was very lucky to have such a kind brother. Next time, Hilary again grabbed what she wanted from Joseph. Immediately Joseph shouted, 'NO, ask nicely.' She shouted, 'Please.' He said pleadingly, 'That's not nicely,' holding the car high up. She said, without shouting this time, 'Please can I have it?' 'Yes.' Hilary was learning from her brother the social rituals involved in negotiating what she wanted. Joseph was actively helping this process. He had also learned to use the adult intervention from the time before. Adults are important in helping children to learn and resolve conflicts. Children use adult strategies in developing their own. Here, Joseph used his father's mode of intervention in a similar situation. If the situation had again broken down, he might well have called for adult help. This is more advanced than 'hitting', but is often seen as 'telling tales'. Initially, adults can help children by demonstrating conflict-removing strategies. The next stage is to act as chairperson while the children argue things out.

Some brothers and sisters seem to relate to one another as 'friends' most of the time. They actively seek each other's company and negotiate well most of the time, protect each other and extend each other. For example, three-year-old William was afraid of the dark. Each evening his mother would tell him a story, tuck him in and leave him with books to look at. Before he settled he wanted to go to the lavatory. He was afraid to go on his own at that time of night. Five-and-a-half-year-old Hannah would wait for him to call, take him and tuck him back in. They enjoyed this nightly ritual which began when she moved to her own separate bedroom. It was during this period that the children began to play with each other when they woke (early) in the mornings, rather than waking their parents.

Other brothers and sisters seem to relate to each other more because they have to so so than as participants in a primarily friendly situation.

Groups

The ability to get on with people is one important part of mixing with other children. This means being able to hold on to your own ideas, to negotiate them, modify them when appropriate and share them. This requires skill! Zick Rubin (1983) suggests that there are four ways in which children need to develop skills in getting on with other children. These are:

1 To be able to gain entry into a group.
2 To be approving and supportive of one's peers.
3 To manage conflicts appropriately.
4 To exercise sensitivity and tact.

In the examples so far, Tom was supportive to Ella, Hannah was supportive to William, and Joseph was supportive to Hilary. Joseph managed and resolved a conflict situation appropriately. Hilary responded sensitively and tactfully to her brother's efforts. Tom, Hannah and Joseph were all sensitive to a younger sibling's needs.

The examples which follow show Rubin's (1983) four strategies in action.

In a nursery school, a group of children was playing pirates. The pirate ship was a scrambling net on a prism-shaped climbing frame. The game involved climbing the 'rigging' and, when another ship was spotted from afar, rushing out and capturing treasure from it, and returning with the booty. The enemy ship would be an agreed place where there was a pile of leaves. The leaves were then brought back as booty. The children were predominatly four years of age — four-year-old James was the pirate leader. Three-year-old Alice wanted to join in. She watched from a distance, walking round the edge of the playground. She approached and stood hopefully at the foot of the climbing frame/pirate ship. She was ignored. She began to climb the net with the others, smiling at her success. As James shouted, 'Ahoy there — a ship. Let's go!' and scrambled down, hotly pursued by the others shouting 'Let's go!', she imitated them. She had been watching for long enough to know that she needed to pick up leaves from the pile. She had successfully joined the game. William Corsaro's work (1979) suggests that Alice's tactics were typical of successful 'access strategies' for entering into a game. She encircled the game, made careful 'verbal overtures', joining in with the other children's 'Let's go!', did similar things to them, and so was not rejected.

This contrasts with four-year-old Mathilde, who wanted to join a group of children in the home corner. She tried to walk in through the door, saying, 'Can I play?' 'No,' shouted the other children in chorus, and shut the door on her. She had not had the opportunity to encircle, and her opening conversation invited rejection. Corsaro's (1979) work suggests that children need to use 'similar behaviour' in order to be accepted. Mathilde could not see what was behind the door, so she was not in a position to engage in similar behaviour in her actions, or to back this up with remarks like, 'We're moving the furniture, aren't we?' William Corsaro calls this kind of remark 'reference to affiliation'.

The way that the classroom is set out has implications for the way that children are able to relate to other children. The home corner, as Sara Smilansky's work (1968) suggested, is an area where quarrels quickly develop, and where children are often rejected from games. It may be that the influence of the nativist model, and the psychodynamic framework with its emphasis on children developing freely in an imaginative world of their own, could in fact be holding back the development of group play in the home corner. High walls may cut children off from imaginative games, and impede the access strategies they need to develop. A feeling of being behind walls can be created where the walls are low enough for the children outside the game to watch it from a distance before joining in.

In the following chapter on the ability to decentre, there are many examples which are relevant to the significant other children in any child's life. Group play offers children the opportunity to see things from other people's points of view. It also offers the child possibilities to experiment with the manipulation of others.

Catherine Garvey (1977) points out that the 'feature of control' is an important one in the formation of children's peer relationships.

Three-year-old Lindsey wants her three-year-old friend Barbara to be a horse. She controls Barbara. Four-year-old Terry wants four-year-old Alex to be a dog. He controls Alex. Six-year-old Hannah wants to play 'Being rich in the old-fashioned days'. She is the Nanny and controls five-year-old Anna. Six-year-old Dominic leads his gang. He captures six-year-old Michael, makes him a prisoner and holds him at gun-point. He controls Michael. Controlling and being controlled, leading and being led, finding out what is acceptable (and negotiating what is), are important aspects of group play.

In chapter 5 on Representation further examples of group play have been given. Adults often find large groups difficult to justify as educationally worthwhile. Some children tend to be involved in this sort of activity almost to the exclusion of any other if given the choice. In the examples in this chapter, and in chapter 5 on Representation and chapter 8 on Decentration, it emerges that group play is an important but undervalued aspect of what early childhood education can offer. Adults need to develop skills in encouraging and promoting this.

At a workshop in a college of education, teachers involved in an in-service course worked with children aged three to five years old from a local nursery school. Four-year-old Gavin started to put large wooden bricks round the edge of the room. Other children copied. Adults intervened when quarrels broke out, or if other equipment which children were using needed to be moved. Soon there was an enclosure of bricks round the whole room. Children began to move around them as if they were stepping stones. About 15 children had become involved in this joint activity. Adults had taken a supportive role, letting children watch until they were 'ready' to join in, altering the physical environment in discussion with the children.

These examples refer to the least adult-dominated aspects of group work with significant other children. Group times, when children come together for stories, music, singing, dancing, or physical education, are more adult-dominated. These can be difficult times for a considerable proportion of children, particularly in the earliest years. Chapter 6 on Language quotes the work of Gordon Wells (1981) which helps us to see why this may be so, and suggests ways in which teachers might develop successful strategies. So far as this chapter is concerned, it is sufficient to say that sitting with a friend often helps children to settle into a group time most easily. The comfort of sitting with a friend is a powerful support.

Partnerships

The Oxford studies (Sylva *et al.*, 1980) point out the importance of two children playing in partnership. It is these relationships which seem best to promote high level play.

In the example of Lindsey and Barbara, two three-year-olds playing horses together, Lindsey puts a long belt around Barbara's waist and 'leads' her. She rehearses what she is going to say so that Barbara is in on the script.

''I say, 'Whoa there!' don't I, and you go, 'Neigh', don't you, and then I pat you and I give you some hay, don't I, and you bend down like this, and you eat it, don't you?'' Then they act out the scene. This helps the children to plan their story in advance, to be clear about the theme and their roles in it.

It is interesting to note that at this time, both Lindsey and Barbara showed interest in things that could be made to encircle. The belt surrounds Barbara's waist. Early friendships are said to be fleeting; one possibility is that they may be based on shared interests and that when these change, the friendship loses its base. After all, the basis of any friendship lies in having shared interests.

It is also interesting that this game was based on a shared experience. The class had been taken to see the police stables, and had been shown the harnesses. The game centred primarily around harnessing and unharnessing a horse. Shared interests and experiences are fundamental aspects of early partnerships.

Six-year-olds Dominic and Michael had both seen *The A-Team* on television. They were acting out a shared secondary experience with a lot of 'stop-go' in this game: careful play punching, holding at gun-point, kicking to the ground. No one gets hurt. This is the sort of game which adults find difficult to allow. There is a tendency to think such play is boyish. This kind of play when indulged in by girls tends to be firmly squashed. In fact, the skill which lies in not hurting each other, the refinement and variety of movement, the planning together, rehearsing and carrying out of the plan, is not unlike the processes of draft, revise, redraft, refine which are involved in story-writing. It also links with Vygotsky's assertion that higher levels of human functioning arise out of early social relationships. In the Oxford Preschool Research Project, Kathy Sylva *et al.* (1980) suggest that rumbustious rough and tumble play does not exercise the intellect. This is true, but it is important to recognise any sophistication which may have been introduced. The kind of play that Michael and Dominic were involved in was not simply rumbustious. It was helping the children to develop on a variety of levels.

Conclusion

This chapter has explored significant people in a child's life — some in the family, some outside it, some chosen by the child, some not. Both adults and children are important, and both family and those in contact with the family are critical in the child's development. The more professional workers in statutory and voluntary agencies concerned with the child's family work together, the better for the child.

Meeting a variety of other children is also important, so that the child develops the ability to form relationships, which may be deep, or of the kind which are necessary simply to cope with everyday living together.

8 The Ability to Decentre

The encouragement of the ability to decentre is crucial to early childhood education. It involves the child in being able to see situations from other points of view, and to empathise with other people. In order to have moral values, and in order that these should be reflected in moral standards of action, it is essential to see situations and people from points of view other than one's own. Decentration is also crucial for the development of acceptable social behaviour. Since it is such an important area, it pervades this book, but in this chapter its importance is highlighted.

Some theoretical considerations regarding the process of decentration

Until recently, it was thought that young children were unable to put themselves into the position of someone else to any great extent. The influence of Jean Piaget's work (1968) led early childhood education to see children under five as 'intellectually egocentric' rather than selfish. Nursery teachers were trained to become skilled in 'diverting' children, rather than attempting what was considered to be impossible — that is, trying to get the child to look at a situation from another child's point of view.

However, one can think of many situations which did not quite fit in with this blanket view that the child was 'egocentric' until five years. For example, four-year-old Wally had been unhappy when settling into school himself. He took three-year-old Peter by the hand and cuddled him when he saw that he was about to cry on his first day. He knew what it was like to be 'new' and could empathise. Six-year-old Vicky and three-year-old Mark were eating ice-cream. Vicky dropped hers and cried. Mark offered her some of his. He knew the 'tragedy', as it seemed to him, of dropping an ice-cream — it had happened to him previously. So practical experience does not seem to back the hypothesis in all situations. Margaret Donaldson's work (1978) helps to explain the apparent contradiction. She makes some links between Piaget's notion of egocentricity and the development from this state to that of decentration — seeing things from other viewpoints. She reminds us that children are able to perform at a higher level when they are working in a meaningful context. Piaget's tests presented children with formal tasks (such as his mountain tests) which were not in such a context. Margaret Donaldson distinguishes between disembedded tasks (i.e. abstract tasks, not performed in a realistic situation) and the embedded tasks which confront children in everyday, spontaneous events and situations. The examples of Wally and Mark quoted above are embedded in meaning and so the children could relate to the situations.

Piaget's work is helpful in that it assists in discerning the stage at which children are able to extend their decentration in the meaningful context into the disembedded, formal context. For the early childhood educator, Margaret Donaldson's emphasis helps teachers to concentrate on providing meaningful contexts as far as possible and to encourage the process of decentration by making full use of them, whether they occur in planned or in spontaneous ways.

Margaret Donaldson *et al.* assert that 'Disembedded tasks are not spontaneous, they are 'set' by the adult, and children must in turn 'set' their minds to them with deliberate constraint and self control' (1983, p. 4).

The role of the early childhood educator seems to be that of a bridge from embedded to disembedded tasks, from everyday meanings to situations beyond the immediate here and now. Bruner (1974) would say that early childhood educators are seeking in appropriate ways to take children 'beyond the information given'. Adults can act as interpreters in this in the way they share experiences with children, especially in the way they encourage truly reciprocal discussions with children rather than adult-dominated activities and conversations.

The ability to decentre also means being able to give up what is immediately wanted in order to have the deeper satisfaction of delayed gratifications. Vygotsky asserts (1978) that children are able to do this when they play. They are prepared to give up what they want now in order that the play does not break down. Vygotsky's perspective on play has been further explored in chapter 5 on Representation.

Kellmer Pringle (1980) balances these aspects of decentration in her assertion that children need both to be given to and to give back. Adults must give love, security, praise, recognition and new experiences. Decentration requires children increasingly to take responsibility for others and themselves. Quality in relationships has been stressed by the theories of Bowlby (1958) and Erikson (1963). Bowlby stressed the need for a constant loving figure who was continually present during the early years. Erikson, through his picture of the 'eight phases of man', emphasised that from a basic sense of trust in the first year, self-esteem emerges in the second. Each stage represents an identity crisis to be overcome. Some children learn to distrust, which leads to lack of self-control, as a result of 'a meagre experience of receiving' in their early days. The quality of early relationships is the key. Although these theories see human development more in terms of an 'unfolding' of the child's innate propensities, either supported or damaged by relationships, they link with the interactionist theories to the extent that meaningful relationships are of importance. The interactionist theories place more emphasis on the reciprocity of the relationships, which are potentially partnerships. At times the adult leads and at times the child. Each takes note of and responds to the other's actions and words. This is the emphasis in the empirical evidence put forward, for example, by Margaret Donaldson *et al.* (1983) or Gordon Wells (1981).

In this section some theoretical considerations about the process of decentration have been explored. The picture emerges whereby the child needs to be actively encouraged by adults to decentre, through meaningful everyday situations; through play and reciprocal discussions; and through teacher-led activities which carefully bridge the gulf from the child's own initiatives, ideas and feelings to those aspects of knowledge with which the teacher wants the child to make contact and integrate into what he or she already knows. While children need to be given love, security, new experiences, praise and recognition, they also need to give by taking increasing responsibility for themselves and others. The example of Matthew (page 138) shows how he was encouraged to discuss his feelings about being responsible for the baby when he was tired.

An important part of the process of decentration lies in the way adults help children to link what they are doing, thinking and feeling with what others are doing, thinking and feeling. The need to be able to do both continues through life. In the section which follows, the emphasis shifts to how to encourage children to decentre.

The appropriate encouragement of decentration

It is one thing for children to be able to decentre, or to empathise with others. It is another to act on this ability. Three guidelines emerge from the last section which help the early childhood educator to encourage children to use their emerging competence in decentration.

1   Children need to experience sensitivity on the part of significant others towards their own intentions, ideas and feelings if they are increasingly to respond to others in this way, and to formulate generalised principles which hold whatever the circumstances.
2   Children need adults to help them make links from the spontaneous event to the teacher-led context, in which language becomes central. Throughout life, there needs to be a balance between the disembedded and the embedded, as new learning occurs. In this way principles of thinking and behaviour begin to develop.
3   Children need to mix with other children in meaningful ways. One of the most meaningful contexts for young children is in play. During play children initiate, experiment, reflect, practise, negotiate and 'become' at their own pace.

These three guidelines are now taken in turn and examples given which show the role of the adult in encouraging or discouraging decentration.

Experiencing sensitivity from others

The first guideline is that children need to experience sensitivity on the part of significant others towards their own intentions, ideas and feelings, if they are increasingly to respond to others in this way. They begin to formulate generalised principles which hold whatever the circumstances.

Three-year-old Amandip is beginning to use English in school. He is enjoying the fact that he can express himself in Punjabi and English. He chatters throughout group time and requests songs and sings them solo, because he cannot wait for the group. He wants to answer all the questions the teacher puts to the group of children. He is irrepressible. His teacher does not stop him, she encourages him, bringing in other children's contributions around his. She recognises his 'explosion' in English, but she does gently insist that the group finishes one song before he suggests another. In the following example, the child's ability to think about everyone present at the tea-table is not encouraged.

Four-year-old Peter had a friend to tea and his mother joined in. There were soon only two scones left and Peter assumed that he and his friend would have them. His mother made no comment. Peter was not being helped to think about the problem of three people and only two scones. In a sense, his mother was holding back the development of decentration by not raising this.

This contrasts with six-year-old Nikolai whose mother thanked him for thinking of her by offering her one of his sweets. She praised his kindness (i.e. decentration) but did not take one, thereby encouraging him to take such a risk again!

Three-and-a-half-year-old Matthew and his baby sister went with his parents to supper at the house of some friends. He was used to sleeping at other houses and happily went to bed upstairs. His father asked him to call out if the newly-born baby started to cry. He agreed. A few minutes later he appeared downstairs crying and saying, 'I don't want to.' His parents did not know what he meant — but it emerged that he did not want to tell the adults if the baby cried. He was happy to sleep upstairs, but did not want to think about the baby. The parents reassured him and he was asleep in five minutes. His mother said that at home he took pride in telling her when the baby had woken up in order to help her. He was tired and in a different setting, but the adults were sensitive to him.

The example of Matthew contrasts with that of Peter in that the family discussions are reciprocal and at times abrasive, but adults are also sensitive to his ideas, feelings and intentions and act accordingly. Peter was not encouraged to discuss who should have the last scones.

The role of the adult in bridging the gap through language

The second guideline for the encouragement of decentration is that children need adults to help them make links from the spontaneous event to the teacher-led context, in which language becomes central. Throughout life, there needs to be a balance between the disembedded and the everyday context.

Six-year-old Jenny asked for another pancake but there was none left. She was angry. Her mother reminded her that she had had two and that there were no more eggs. She pointed out that in Ethiopia it would be difficult to get *any* eggs, flour, or milk, and this led to an interesting discussion on why and how food ought to be taken to people. Jenny had watched Bob Geldof on TV. Every day for a time she began to invite discussion about her meals in relation to low technology cooking, food availability, climatic conditions and so on. Jenny's mother had helped her to link some difficult concepts for a six-year-old to grasp from a television programme to a spontaneous situation which had great meaning for her. Gordon Wells (1983) points out that home talk is particularly good in this respect. He suggests that teachers need to develop this linking strategy in schools.

In the following examples a teacher and parent are working together in this way. At school, the teacher was doing a project on 'flowers'. She had an interest table full of them, with some that children could take apart and look at under magnifying glasses. Three-year-old Melissa enjoyed putting things inside others (a topological, spatial schema in Piaget's theory). She homed in on this interest table, and began putting flowers into vases with gusto. At home time the teacher explained this interest to her mother and asked her if she would like to take the pot of flowers home to follow up the school work. The mother had had problems in getting Melissa to come to table at mealtimes because she always wanted to bring her toys with her. She found that by asking Melissa to put some flowers (even weeds from the garden) in a vase on the table she could overcome this problem. Delighted, she told the teacher about this in school next day. This marked a turning-point for Melissa who began to help her mother prepare the table for meals at home and then sat down readily. She had begun to decentre a little more and to make the link from bringing a toy to the table to making the objects on the table relevant to the meal. It was not purely what she wanted, but what was needed at mealtimes.

Seven-year-old Anthony purposefully scratched a mark on a wooden table. The teacher reprimanded him and told him that he must not spoil the table in that way. He was crestfallen. So that he didn't feel that she had rejected him, but only what he had done, she praised him when he picked a toy up which might have got crushed on the floor. She was firmly operating on the principle that there should be respect for property in the classroom in a meaningful context for Anthony. Hilda Garrard, formerly of the Froebel Institute, London, calls this 'law with love' (1986). The teacher pointed out that she had cared about the table being spoilt and she was glad that he cared about the toy being crushed. In this way she linked the two events.

The teacher in a class of six-year-olds planned a cookery lesson. The children were to make baked apples in a group of six. They made one for themselves and one extra each to give as a present. Joanna said that she wanted one for her brother and one for her mother. She, the teacher and the other children discussed the fairness of this — and eventually it was decided that she would have to cut up and divide the two apples when she got home. The teacher helped her to think of others, to see the unfair implications of giving her extra apples, and to become involved in the mathematics of division. She was helping her to consider others, justice and mathematics, all in a meaningful embedded context and yet moving slightly away from the immediate towards the disembedded context.

The importance of play

The third guideline for encouraging children to decentre is that children need to mix meaningfully with other children. The section which follows is more extensive than the previous two because it gives an opportunity to explore practical examples of the importance of play, not only in relation to decentration, but also more generally for early childhood education.

Children need variety in the ways in which they mix with other children, ranging from partnerships to groups.

Children need to work with children older and younger, more and less advanced, as well as children operating at the same level. This applies to both partnership and group situations.

Partnerships can involve older and younger children, more and less advanced, or children of the same age or stage. Stage is more important than age. The following examples show partnerships between two children at different stages.

Five-year-old Hannah reads each night to three-year-old William. The books he enjoys are at the level she can read 'approximately', from her knowledge of the story and the picture clues. She is thinking of stories that he enjoys, but she is gaining satisfaction from the giving by using her latest learning in a meaningful setting. Diana Leat (1977) sees voluntary work (usually seen as advanced decentring on the part of adults) as requiring components of both giving and receiving to be successful.

Turiel and Weston (1983) demonstrate that children at three can distinguish between between different types of rules. Moral rules (it is wrong to hit) were regarded as unchangeable. Other kinds of rule (you must tidy the room before going out) could be changed.

A different partnership is exemplified between two children at the same stage. Six-year-olds Tom and William were in the garden together. Both are particularly interested in natural science and this had been the basis of a friendship since the age of three. They found a crusader spider and made an assault course for it. They were delighted when it climbed up a pole and along a string they had rigged up. William tried to help it to realise there was another pole for it to climb down. He gently touched it, but the spider bit him. He was interested in this, as there had been discussion in his family for years about whether spiders did bite people. Both boys chatted constantly. 'Let's put a dead fly for him to eat, then he'll come.' 'No, it's got to be in a web.' 'Does he have a web or is he a pouncer?' 'What's a pouncer?' 'He hides and then pounces.' 'Oh!' There was a lot of negotiating. This is give and take of a different kind from that of the first type of partnership. It involves a different kind of looking from various points of view and is very challenging.

At times, partnerships need adult intervention. Four-year-olds Alistair and Stuart made a tune out of circles stuck on stave lines on a board. It was a monotone. The teacher sang it for them, and moved away. Stuart changed it so that it went up at the end, but Alistair did not want to change it. He tried to put the note down again, but Stuart grabbed it and ran off. Alistair gave chase; he was furious. Stuart's mother said, 'Give him back his tune, Stuart.' It was suggested by the teacher that Stuart should start another row underneath Alistair's, going up at the end. She then played this on the xylophone, Alistair played his row and Stuart played his. Here the negotiation broke down and the partnership required adult help. Neither child could decentre without help. The adult could have made Stuart apologise to Alistair, but preferred to give the message that it is more satisfying and produces better results to co-operate rather than fight.

So far, partnerships have been highlighted. One kind of partnership involves an older child helping a younger child, but experiencing great pleasure in doing so. Another involves children at the same stage of development sharing and negotiating their way through a first-hand experience. The third type of partnership showed an adult intervening sensitively when co-operation broke down. There are other sorts of partnership, of course.

Group situations with peers, more and less advanced and at the same stage, are also important during early childhood. Group play involves children in giving up their immediate wishes in order that the game can continue successfully. Vygotsky (1978) sees this as an important attribute. A shoe shop had been set up in the classroom. The family of four-year-old Neelan owns a shop. She watched the teacher pretend to be the shopkeeper and quickly assumed that role. She took younger children, three-year-olds Shazia and Toto, as customers. Certainly she dominated the play, but she was inducting them into what imaginative play is about. They willingly stayed, but could have left at any time. Toto and Shazia needed Neelan to show them how to play 'pretend games', how to take roles and become other people — how to decentre and see other viewpoints.

Anna Maria is another typical three-year-old. The teacher was working with a group of children on the large bricks. They (two girls and two boys) were sitting on them as a table and chairs. Four-year-old Tracy brought a small brick cylinder and said, 'Would you like a tin of beans?' and laughed. The teacher said, 'I'd love some — but I need to open the tin.' She pretended to do this to a rapt audience. Then she asked for a saucepan in which to heat the beans. Sade found a flatter cylinder (a thoroughly appropriate representation of a saucepan). The teacher pretended to pour in the beans and stir. Then she asked for some plates. The children found more bricks and the teacher made toast using rectangular shapes. At this point Anna Maria came in and watched the activity. She came up to the teacher and said triumphantly, 'You're only pretending, you know.' She did not want to join in, she only wanted to watch the game. Three-year-olds need to see high-level imaginative play before being helped into it. This has implications for later work in school. Getting on the inside of roles and themes in imaginative play requires the child to go beyond 'self' and to 'become' other people in other situations in a meaningful context.

Becoming someone else, acting out a role and a theme, requires considerable decentration. The spontaneous 'scripts' which develop during imaginative play are the stuff of later story-writing. This form of play encourages the embryonic sense of audience which will flower later on. Seven-year-old Hannah, three-year-old Christopher and five-year-olds Matthew and William decide to play King Arthur. Only Hannah and William know the story and the game quickly disintegrates. All the children know the story of Robin Hood. Hannah suggests that they play this instead and she co-ordinates the story. There is a lot of discussion: 'You say ''I am hurt'' and I say ''Get up'' ' and so on. The script is agreed and carried out in action. All dress up in clothes from the dressing-up box, with swords. Chris (the youngest) follows. He makes mistakes, goes to the wrong place, kills the 'wrong' person and the other children — mainly Hannah — alert him to what is needed. Interestingly, in games of mixed ages or large groups of children there often seems to be a great deal of rushing about and follow-my-leader activity. Younger children need the stimulation and leadership of more advanced children. Older children need to lead and organise complicated games, with younger children as willing participants. According to Piaget, from the age of approximately eight, the ability to hold in mind several factors in the disembedded context simultaneously develops steadily. If Vygotsky (1978) is correct in his view on zones of potential development, then imaginative group play in

Group play, like partnership play, is important in helping children to decentre.

meaningful (embedded) contexts serves as an opportunity for children in the three to seven age group to start to hold in mind several factors at once. Hannah, if the game is to succeed, needs to help Chris by trying to see his difficulties. She needs to keep William and Matthew happy about Christopher's 'errors', and to negotiate, smooth situations over and make acceptable suggestions. Maid Marion, she points out, when Matthew makes a bid to become leader of the game, is as good at shooting arrows as Robin Hood. After all, Matthew is Robin Hood. He insists that he is a better archer. William supports Hannah. 'It's in the book,' he declares. Hannah gets round this by suggesting that they all surround the Sheriff of Nottingham (a bush in the garden), but do not kill him.

Group play, like partnership play, is important in helping children to develop the ability to decentre. In the example of Neelan's leadership of the group, the importance of mathematics was the focus. Matching, sorting, putting shoes and feet into a one to one correspondence are some instances of the mathematical situations involved. In the example of Anna Maria, she needed to grasp the drama of the position — how to 'become' someone else, in a different situation. In the example of Hannah, William, Christopher and Matthew, adherence to a text was required. The correct version of Robin Hood's story was demanded by the participants, who willingly submitted to its requirements. This links with the partnerships in which Jenny became involved with her mother in environmental issues, Melissa became involved in artistic presentation of meals (functional art), Tom and William were involved in studying natural science, Alistair and Stuart were composing music. Every area of the curriculum contributes to fostering decentration in young children. The broader the curriculum the better.

In these examples, adults have only intervened when relationships, roles, themes, shared constructions of meanings and so on broke down. Adults supported or extended the children's intentions or initiatives. They did not 'take over', nor did they leave children to flounder. They were at hand to act sensitively as situations developed. If children are not given opportunities to experiment and negotiate, share, argue, or agree, they do not become skilled in these important areas. However, situations break down rapidly with young children. When this happens, adults are vital in order to curb escalations and fights which go beyond the experimental. In these examples also, adults valued spontaneous events which clarified children's intentions and helped them to extend learning. Strategies used by adults were making appropriate provision (Neelan), conversations (Anna Maria), leaving the children alone when roles and themes were developing (Hannah, William, Matthew and Christopher), intervening during quarrels which the children were not able to resolve (Alistair and Stuart).

Conclusion

The ability to empathise and to see things from different points of view develops in competency throughout early childhood. The process of decentration requires active help from adults, and the experiences which come from mixing with a range of children. The implications of the process are found in every area of knowledge. In this chapter, some of the areas of knowledge included environmental studies (Jenny), natural science (Melissa, Tom and William), literature (Hannah and William), music (Alistair and Stuart), dramatic play (Hannah, William, Matthew and Christopher) and mathematics (Neelan).

9 The Commonalities and Differences between People

This chapter looks at how childhood educators should approach commonalities and differences between children, especially those from minority or disadvantaged groups. It uses case studies and examples of class, gender, physical disability, race and religious issues and explores these in relation to six guiding principles.

The education system periodically identifies special groups

One of the problems educators have always encountered is how to work with individual children within a whole group. Even within the family, this can be difficult. Certainly, only children tend statistically to 'get on' academically, and to be successful in careers later on. They are given very individual help by their families. It is difficult to achieve such a highly individual approach in the classroom, within a group setting.

What is clear is that common treatment of all children is disastrous for many, and not even ideal for children from the dominant class or ethos, or who are of high ability.

Policy-makers and educational theorists have, over the years, identified particular groups of children whose needs have been significantly ignored. In the 1960s, studies such as Douglas's (1964) alerted educators to the fact that working-class children were not being successful in the education system. This led to attempts to remedy the situation through compensatory education focusing on cognition. Three useful features emerged from the compensatory movement. Programmes with lasting impact were found to involve the family, to be geared to individuals within the group and to be structured in a consistent way. Because the whole family was involved, account was taken of what the child came to school able to do. The child's background and home experiences were valued. Observing the child and using what the child was naturally doing was also valued. Examples of this approach can be seen in Constance Kamii's work in the Ypsilanti Early Education Programme in the USA (Kamii and Devries, 1977), and Lin Poulton, George and Teresa Smith's work in the Red House Project in West Yorkshire (part of the Halsey 1972 Studies on Educational Priority) and subsequent work in Hampshire (Poulton, 1979) together with the Leverhulme /Gulbenkian Research Project directed by Chris Athey at the Froebel Institute, London, 1972–6, in Britain.

The most salient conclusion from all this work was that it is not so much that working-class children need an entirely different education, it is rather that they need more individual and sensitive treatment within the mainstream of education, and a more appropriate valuation of the contributions made by their families in their education.

In the late 1970s, a different 'disadvantaged' group was identified. The Warnock Report (DES, 1978) served as a catalyst for thinking about children's special needs, and how best to promote their development. The 1981 Education Act, which arose out of this report, said:

> A child has a special need if he/she has a learning difficulty significantly greater than the majority of children of the age, or a disability which prevents the use of educational facilities of a kind generally provided in schools for children of that age.

This broad definition covers one in six children at any one time and attempts to avoid labelling children in medical terms, grouping them on the basis of educational need. Warnock proposed a continuum model of identifying needs rather than gross categorisation (e.g. not either 'hearing', 'partially-hearing', or 'deaf', but regarding all as 'hearing-impaired' with varying needs and degrees of handicap along a continuum). This gives more flexibility. As with the more successful approaches to combating class bias, the emphasis was, and is, on integrating children with special needs into mainstream education rather than segregating them and providing special education.

Warnock emphasised the importance of the early years and of partnership with parents. The continuum model potentially helps to rekindle individuality by a more sensitive and appropriate treatment of children.

Another focus in the 1980s has been on the needs of children who, until very recently, as Brian Jackson (1979) points out, have received a strong implicit message from the educational system: 'You do not exist.' However, gradually children from different minority ethnic groups are beginning to be acknowledged as needing more appropriate help in their development. This is a further example of the trend to rekindle individuality.

Awareness of race issues leads to distinctions being made between separating the parts from the whole, assimilating the parts into the whole, and integrating the parts and the whole.

More recently still the work of Michelle Elliott (1985) and others is motivating educators to focus also on children who are abused or neglected physically, emotionally, or sexually.

Issues surrounding gender have, in the mid 1980s, also received more attention by educators involving the different kinds of help needed by boys and girls. This focuses on the varying achievements of boys and girls in different curriculum areas and careers, and the extent to which these derive from stereotypes relating to gender, or the influence of powerful sex-role models in the family and society in general. The emphasis is on neutralising and expanding tightly-set sex roles in order to free boys and girls to take on broader and wider roles in life.

Guiding principles in the education of minority or neglected groups

It is understandable that some of those involved in early childhood education at worst regard the increased emphasis on different groups as a new 'fad', and at best find it difficult and confusing to put each new focus of social policy into practice. Some principles of approach are needed, and what follows is a first attempt to define such principles by way of an expansion of guidelines already in existence for one of these special groups, namely minority ethnic groups.

At an Organisation Mondiale pour l'Education Prescolaire (OMEP) conference in London in 1983, Yvonne Conolly spoke on the subject of the multicultural classroom in the early years of education. She set out six fundamentally-important guiding principles. These can also help in the exploration of issues surrounding the needs of any child who is not straightforwardly part of the majority group in the education system.

As more and more differing groups emerge, it becomes increasingly clear that the central aim of the mainstream of education needs to be to emphasise individuals, and to work in partnership with the family. Otherwise, insensitive and inappropriate work results, which leads to underachievement in many children. Yvonne Conolly, like the early childhood pioneers, stresses what children have in common. She believes that, 'A good education is a good education for all.' This, for her, is the starting point in working with children as unique individuals. At the conference she asserted that:

1 The parts of the whole are the whole.
2 Children need a sense of belonging.
3 Children must not be placed in a dilemma about their own sense of worth.
4 People must be allowed to identify themselves, and others should not do it for them.
5 Each of us should look at our assumptions and attitudes in relation to the notion of respect for others. This requires inspecting our actions and values. It involves stereotyping and attitude awareness.
6 That the natural 'stranger fear' of people needs to be overcome through positive strategies of action.

One of the difficulties facing the early childhood educator is the increasing number of groups identified as particularly needing individual help. It is helpful to the educator to have these six guiding principles which can be applied to any child in a minority group, or indeed to any child.

The examples which follow illustrate each of Yvonne Conolly's assertions. They cover class, race, gender, special needs and religion. Abuse is not covered, but this important subject can be followed up in specialist books on the subject, including Michelle Elliot's (1985).

1 The parts of the whole are the whole

The first principle, 'The parts are the whole', means that the parts cannot be treated in isolation from the whole, nor absorbed into a whole, but should be respected as distinct

aspects of the whole, contributing to as well as taking from
it. To turn this guiding principle into practice, it is helpful
to identify three sub-themes, as follows:

(a) Integration is preferable to assimilation.
(b) The whole must understand the parts as well as the
    parts understanding the whole.
(c) Emphasis should be on commonalities and identifying
    diversity in a positive light.

(a) Integration, not assimilation

One of the problems is that the whole tends to assimilate
parts into it, rather than to integrate them. There is an enormous difference between assimilation and integration. The
problem of assimilation is that it demands of the person the
rejection of his or her present self in order to become a part
of the majority — 'like everyone else'. For example, in the
UK in the 1950s and 1960s the desire of educators was to
teach deaf children (as they were then called) to talk
through the pure oral method. Hearing aids, lip-reading, use
of residual hearing were emphasised. Deaf children, it was
agreed, should not be deprived of the right to oral language.
They should be helped to be as much like the mainstream
majority as possible. Michael was an adult brought up in
this way. He was a good lip-reader and his speech was clear.
He attended a summer theatre school for the deaf. He related
best to the hearing people on the course, but found it difficult to follow their conversations except on an individual
basis. He was ill at ease with most of the deaf-course
members, unless they used oral language. He could not use
British Sign Language. From an early age Michael's education had asked him to deny his deafness, and to overcome it
so that he could live a 'normal' life. In fact, because he was
profoundly deaf, he was not quite part of the hearing world,
but he had rejected the 'deaf' world. He was between the
two, and this contributed to his deep loneliness with few
close friends.

   Jim, on the other hand, was able to use British Sign
Language and oral language. He, like Michael, was profoundly deaf. He had attended mainstream schools and was
at university — but he had always belonged to groups of the
deaf at which he had learned to sign. He had friends who
were deaf and friends who were not. His bilingualism helped

to develop close friendships with both groups. He said that with hearing people he often became very tired with the concentration and effort required to listen hard and to lip-read, especially in group conversations. He relaxed with deaf friends where he could sign. Interestingly, Jim's first remark when he met anyone at the summer school was, 'Are you deaf or hearing?' He was at ease with his deafness. He did not try to deny it. He did not want to. His only bit-terness was that hearing people were so insensitive to the needs of the minority group to which he belonged. He felt a privileged member of his group, as he was bilingual. His parents had fought hard to help him succeed in spite of all the obstacles posed by insensitive and inflexible systems.

Michael had been *assimilated* into the mainstream; Jim had been *integrated*. In Michael's case, as in the case of the children Brian Jackson (1979) describes, 'You do not exist' was the message. Fitting in with the mainstream becomes the only option. It means rejecting what makes you dif-ferent from most people. It means denying your 'special-ness', your uniqueness, so that the parts must be absorbed into the whole.

In Jim's case, the part has been allowed to keep its par-ticular aspect. However, it has been split off from the whole and left to exist in isolation. It has been encouraged to be part of the whole appropriately, through being valued. The part, in this situation, is the whole.

The integrated approach can be seen in the need to value and encourage the child's mother tongue where a different language is used in the home from that used in the school. It is also present in the need to value dialects which relate to class and regional differences. It is present in the need for children of minority ethnic groups to know about their own language, cultural roots and religious ideas and for the educator to value these. For example, three-year-old Pratima came to school with her grandmother, who spoke Punjabi. The teacher managed to greet her in Punjabi. Shortly after, Pratima became distressed and fearful. It was clearly something to do with her shoes and shoe-bag. Grandmother could not speak English to explain to the teacher, and the teacher's grasp of Punjabi was too limited. Fortunately, the school was following an integration rather than assimilation approach, and Punjabi was sufficiently valued in the school for there to be a Punjabi-speaking member of staff. She was asked to help and the situation was instantly resolved — Pratima's tears vanished. The wrong shoe-bag was on her peg; hers was found. Pratima's English was developing very well — but in a stress situation she could not use it and it would be inappropriate to expect her to do so. No one uses the latest piece of learning when under stress.

An assimilatory approach (needing no extra resources) can be seen conflicting with an integrated approach (requiring extra resources) in the following example. Five-year-old Rebecca, a Down's syndrome child, attended a local nursery school. Before school entry, she regularly had speech therapy and physiotherapy. Her parents were told that because she had been judged capable of going to the nursery school, this was no longer necessary and could not be offered. In short, she was being treated like everyone else and her specialness denied — a case of assimilation, not integration. The head of the nursery school and the parents complained about this. The speech therapist and physiotherapist agreed to give guidance to the school and home on what Rebecca needed in these areas. She needed plenty of opportunities to blow, suck and chew. She needed opportunities for fine manipulation. Fortunately, the parents and head were able to insist that Rebecca was seen as a part within the whole, requiring specialist help as part of the integration rather than absorption into the whole. Later the local primary school, which Rebecca's brothers and sisters had attended, refused her entry. The head wanted to accept her, but on the basis of integration and not assimilation. As the head could not be assured that essential extra resources would be available (specialist staffing and equipment), she refused to take Rebecca.

(b) The need to understand the parts

Jim's situation (above) raises another important issue if integration is to be achieved. He was bitter that the mainstream did not try to see things from his point of view, or understand his world, his experiences, his beliefs. He felt that he was required to make all the effort. He had managed to become integrated because of his family. His parents were hearing and knew how to 'force' the mainstream to listen to their requests.

James, two years old, was profoundly deaf; so were his parents. He signed at home. At the special school for the deaf which he attended, he was not allowed to sign. He was required to use oral language. His home language was denied in school, rather than being valued. He is not in such a difficult position as Michael for he is learning about both signing (at home) and oral language (in school). Nevertheless, here the whole (the school) was refusing to understand or acknowledge the part (the home). This contrasts with Pratima, where the mother tongue was valued and encouraged.

It is not so easy for 'the parts' to be understood by and to change 'the whole' if they are not yet part of the whole, and remain outside it. This is reflected in the paucity of the numbers of people from minority ethnic groups in positions of power to effect such changes in the current 'whole' of society. Judith Katz (1978) asserts that racism is about the assertion of rights and interests of a particular racial group who assume superiority, however unwittingly, and have power to enforce this to the detriment of other racial groups.

For the parts to be truly part of the whole, the whole must know about and understand the parts and act accordingly. Six-year-old Nahugo's mother takes her to school each day. She walks straight past the other mothers. This upsets William's mother, who feels her smile of greeting is rejected. A friend has recently returned from Japan and explains that in Japan people do not greet each other with a smile in the street. They ignore each other unless there is a verbal greeting. Next day, William's mother verbally greets Nahugo's mother. She looks a little taken aback, but immediately smiles and responds. Thereafter, the two mothers talk to each other each day.

Five-year-old Judith was collecting her school lunch. It was pork. She returned to her place at the table with her meal. The teacher intercepted, asked the dinner lady for an alternative meal without pork and quietly gave it to Judith. 'No one would have known', was the dinner lady's response. She did not worry that Judith's family practised Reformed Judaism, and that they trusted the school to apply the dietary stipulations of the religion. She did not understand the importance of these, and no one had yet made her begin to think that this point needed any attention. She expected Judith to be assimilated into the majority's eating habits rather than to take it on herself to contribute to her integration into school mealtimes.

(c) Emphasis should be on commonalities and identifying diversity positively

Implementing the assertion that the part is the whole is not easy in practice. It requires knowledge of different cultures, history, creeds and disabilities. It is not enough to expect all children to study the dominant culture, history, or religion, as this does not lead to understanding between parts and whole; so there is no whole, only parts. Looking at the commonalities between, for example, different religions and philosophies helps communication, understanding and respect for differences, which can then be valued as part of the diversity of the parts within the whole.

For example, every religion emphasises a sense of awe and wonder in the way people relate to the universe. Every religion addresses itself to the celebration of this. Every religion involves its participants in a coming together as a group around something considered by that group to be of worth. Rachel Gregory (1982, p.6) explores the notion of 'Worthship' which has become shortened to 'worship'.

Five-year-old Anthea attended a Church of England primary school. During assembly the head told the children about Doubting Thomas, who had the opportunity to believe in Jesus, but did not take it. This placed Anthea in a dilemma. Her mother was agnostic, her father was an atheist. Both had had the opportunity to believe and had rejected it. What did this make her parents in the eyes of the school and church? Anthea dealt with the situation by keeping secret throughout her education the fact of her parents' rejection of Christianity as a means of retaining her self-worth at school. In fact, in many respects she received a sounder religious education from her parents than other children in the school. She experienced with her family a sense of awe and wonder about the universe (her father was a scientist). She learned about celebration at family gatherings when African music was played and danced to. She learned about 'worthship' in family gatherings which involved discussion of matters of worth — starvation, poverty, peace, human rights and repression. This example demonstrates that organised religion is not the only means by which children are given a sound religious education.

The following examples also show commonalities and positively-viewed diversity in religious settings. Six-year-old Ovo's family were pantheists, believing in spirits in the trees and plants. He, of all the children in his class, was able to understand the North American Indian tribes' relationship with their natural surroundings during the class project on this. Five-year-old Margaret was brought up as a Roman Catholic. She could understand that five-year-old Diana wore a Star of David just as she wore a crucifix. Four-year-old Sadiq was taken to Westminster Abbey on a school outing. He thought the statues had no clothes on as they were carved in stone, and saw them as rude. His mother was fascinated by the outing and explained to the teacher, who was a Methodist, that in the Muslim mosque there are no statues. These examples demonstrate the problems of assuming majority views. All these children bring different religious experiences, although it is to be hoped that each will sense awe and wonder, will celebrate, will experience worthship in some form.

Studying different cultures may initially look hopelessly complicated, especially for children in the first seven years, until it is remembered that everyone eats, everyone likes to present food attractively, using crockery, or equivalent tools to eat with, sitting in a variety of ways. Everyone sleeps, on beds, in hammocks, bunks and so on. Everyone needs protection from heat or cold resulting in a need for clothing — and everyone needs shelter. Bruner's 1965 curriculum project *Man — A Course of Study* (Bruner, 1972, p. 56) was an interesting early attempt at this approach. The exhibition 'Come Over to My House' (ILEA, 1976) had a similar theme.

The different ways that people tackle these aspects of life then become fascinating and important. They lead to respect for differences through geographical or regional variations, or for historic reasons, which help understanding of cherished traditions and rituals.

2 Developing a sense of belonging

Everyone needs roots and to feel that they belong to a group. Fostering a sense of belonging in an individual or minority also helps the majority by encouraging the ability to decentre — something which is very important for young children, as shown in the last chapter.

An example of this is shown with one class of six-year-olds. Ufoma had never been to Nigeria, but with the other children she had learnt about Nigerian housing, climate and crops. On ceremonial days her family always wore traditional costumes and she brought these to school. Her mother cooked some traditional food and sent it to school. The teacher showed the children the ingredients and cooked the food in school with them. She invited an African drummer to visit and everyone danced. Ufoma's roots were being publicly valued. She only partly knew them. The other children began to understand why Ufoma liked hot, spicy food and wore the clothes she sometimes wore, and they respected the way she could dance. She was more popular than before because the children could put her more in context. She was no longer just 'different'. She was special and unique — and yet like them in important ways. Ufoma herself had more sense of the roots to which she belonged. However, the black child has no choice about belonging to a 'black group'.

It is important that any child feels pride in the group to which he/she belongs. This applies equally to Jim, Michael, Anthea and Ufoma. Children need to be able to put themselves in meaningful contexts, where everything links. A focus on the commonality between people, which in turn highlights positive variations and diversity, is helpful.

3 Encouraging a sense of worth

Self-worth, self-esteem and self-confidence are probably the most important aspects of human development. The way that people feel about themselves affects the way that they seem to others.

Maureen Stone asserts (1981) that self-esteem, or self-worth, is only damaged if the child is rejected or not valued by the group to which he/she wishes to 'belong'. She points out that if the child does not value the school's opinions, self-esteem is not necessarily affected. Anthea rejected the school's opinion of non-believers and retained her self-worth. Three-year-old Nasreen was in a more complex situation. She was from a Muslim family, but her father was an alcoholic and so her family was particularly disapproved of by the Muslim community. She had been brought to school as usual by her older sister. As the teacher greeted her on arrival, a neighbour brought his child in. He said something in Punjabi to Nasreen and mimed a drinking movement. As he turned to go she stuck out her tongue at his back and went to the teacher and put her hand in hers. She knew the teacher valued her, and would not be disapproving towards her family. In this case, the school was supporting her sense of self-worth.

The way that people feel about themselves affects the way they seem to others.

Four-year-old Kuang's and six-year-old Ming's mother was British, their father was Chinese. Their parents helped them to understand Chinese culture through the furniture and decor in the home, the food they sometimes ate, the emphasis on stories and Chinese ideas about health, acupuncture, Tai Chi and herbal medicines. They also knew about the British cultural setting from their mother and from school. Kuang took pride in showing his school friends how to write 'mountain' in Chinese. His parents helped him be proud of what he was, half Chinese and half British.

Some children have to ask themselves who they are more than others and this can put them in a dilemma about their own sense of worth. Anthea could hide the minority stance her parents took. Ufoma could not. A positive sense of self-worth is the right of any child and it is the responsibility of the early childhood educator to encourage this, especially among those children whose sense of worth might be challenged by the majority.

4 Allow and encourage self-identification rather than labelling

Knowing who you are, and being at ease with yourself, is closely linked with self-worth. Part of being able to do this lies in the way children can put themselves into context. 'Who am I?' is an important question, which all people ask of themselves at some point in their life.

Children from minority groups are at a disadvantage in this respect — be it a minority ethnic group, a religious group, a disability group, a social class group or a gender group — because others tend to label them.

It is easier for some children to choose their identity than for others. There was no question for Ufoma but that she was one black child in a class of 20 children of West European background. There is often a tendency for the majority to label those from minority groups in a gross way. Peter is 'the blind boy' rather than someone who has as many unique qualities as any sighted child. Ufoma is black or African rather than a child who loves maths and hates gym.

Helping children to identify themselves is probably one of the hardest tasks facing a teacher, and probably the safest and most constructive thing he/she can do is to keep the choices open. Education, to a large extent, is about increasing the choice people have. Michael did not have the choice that Jim had.

Paul Griffin (1986) gives an interesting account of his mother-in-law's priorities for a girl's education in 1925 and her attempts to provide girls with choices. Girls in her curriculum model were to be competent house-keepers, trained for motherhood, and well-read. In this model they had the choice, he argues, of being good at serving their families, their employers, or their country. Girls trained only for careers are reduced in that choice. Serving the family is out of fashion. It is seen as exploitation, or underachievement by women. If Griffin's argument is taken seriously, in the modern context both boys and girls should be educated to have the choice of working in the family, or in employment (Steedman, 1982). Currently, men rarely have the choice of working in the family, and women are in a dilemma about their self-worth if they are in a position to opt for it.

A girl involved in a science activity. Education is about increasing the choice people have.

Education needs to be broad with a wide curriculum. It also needs to avoid stereotyping people into an identity. A teacher on an in-service course in London came from

Yorkshire. She came on a term's secondment. She thought of herself as British, but suddenly everyone began to ask her about Yorkshire. 'Oh! You're from Yorkshire . . .' She began to feel that she was a foreigner. She felt her Yorkshire accent becoming stronger. She found herself wanting to read about the Industrial Revolution and the wool trade. She needed to assert her identity — but it was being chosen for her by others. She was swept along by the way that other people insisted on regarding her. She was being stereotyped.

Girls are typically seen to be bad at mathematics, but gentle and helpful. Boys are typically seen to be slow to read and write, but strong and brave and boisterous. In this section, the need for individuals to assert their own identity is stressed. In the next section, this will be seen to link with the need for each of us, especially those in positions of power, which teachers and nursery nurses in a classroom inevitably are, to inspect their own thinking and examine their fundamental assumptions.

5 Inspecting and examining basic assumptions

Gordon Wells (1983, p. 137) makes the point strongly that basic assumptions need to be examined in relation to class issues. He asserts that:

> Any suggestion that working-class children as a whole are 'disadvantaged' in any absolute or irrevocable sense because their home experience leads them to use language differently, is certainly not appropriate.

He argues that this distracts 'teachers from their obligations to examine their own role in helping children to make a success of the transition from home to school'.

Boy babies are bounced and thrown in the air more. Girls are sung and talked to more and held closer. As they progress, the emphasis for girls is on conformity and neatness. Boys are allowed, and so indirectly encouraged, to be more attention-seeking. The way girls are treated in primary schools is often different, although teachers are frequently unaware of this. This is seen in the brick corner, home corner, in outdoor play and so on. One nursery school head teacher asked, without thinking, for some strong boys to help her move some furniture. A voice piped up beside her, 'And strong girls.' Four-year-old Emily jolted her thinking.

Even the gender of the majority of teachers in primary education has sex-stereotyping implications, not only for the children they teach but for the whole image of the early childhood educator. In the primary school most teachers are women and Carolyn Steedman asserts (1986) that we need to discover 'how, and in what manner, we've been made to fit there' (p. 161). She argues that the middle-class woman is in evidence there as the 'Mother-made-conscious', who does not have to be very intelligent, but in whom 'feeling, intuition, sympathy and empathy is all' (p. 160). No doubt most readers of her article would challenge this sterotype! But the article does put the case for the 'Parent-made-conscious' rather than only the mother in primary schools. It highlights the need for more balanced staffing, with both men and women.

In a nursery school in Southall a teacher took positive steps to try to overcome the stereotype that boys are better at science. She wanted to do some work on electricity with a group of three- and four-year-olds. She took in some battery-powered electric circuits, and was interested to find that only boys sat down to work with them. Two girls came, but there were no seats for them so they went away. Four-year-old Reena came back later. The boys were monopolising the activity. When Reena came back, four-year-old Nisham spread his elbows across the circuits. He was not going to let her in. When he was ready to leave, he called his friend, so that he could take his place. The teacher insisted that Reena must have the place since she had been waiting longest. Other girls began to hover on the outskirts of the activity. The teacher worked consciously to include them, but the girls were having more difficulty. They were pushed away by the boys if they tried to sit down.

A week later the teacher repeated the activity. This time, there was a balance of boys and girls. It was as if the teacher's insistence that the eligibility for doing the activity should be by turn-taking rather than whose friend you are, had had an influence. In the third week, the Christmas tree was decorated — the children put electric fairy lights on it and made up the circuit themselves. This time the girls came first to the activity. On this occasion the teacher worked hard to encourage the few 'hovering' boys to join in. Already, these young children had picked up their sex roles, and were stereotyping themselves and each other. Pretty

lights meant a girl's activity. The situation required
positive strategies by the teacher to neutralise the sex roles
and combat the stereotypes. The teacher needed to inspect
her own thinking and assumptions, but more than that she
needed to take action in relation to it. Being aware of racism
or sexism is not enough. It requires action.

Another crucial area of stereotyping is that which leads to
racism. Three-year-old Sadiq wanted to go in the home corner. The other children refused him entry. Three-year-old
Mary said, 'We don't want Pakis.' The teacher heard, and
confronted the situation directly. She told Mary that she
thought her remark unkind, and that she did not want
anyone in the class to be unkind. She asked Mary what a
Paki was. Mary said, 'Black.' The teacher asked her if Sadiq
was in fact black. She asked Mary what she was. Mary said,
'White.' She asked her if in fact she was white. She then
told Sadiq to join the children in the house. They accepted
him. Later, at group time, she asked the children to look at
the person next to them to see what colour his or her skin
was. The children found a wide range. Then they sang
'Under One Sun' and 'Ten Little Toes'. She stressed the
commonalities and differences between them — all human,
all with toes and skin, but with variations in the shapes of
toes and colour of skin. She made it clear that she valued
each child, and respected them all. She also made it clear
that it was unacceptable that any member of the school
community should not value or respect any other.

Mary's and Sadiq's mothers were both present at the song
time. Both knew the teacher valued and respected their
child, and themselves, and expected the same of them in
school. Sadiq's mother had given him the language of prejudice in describing the Caucasian children as 'Pinkies' in
Urdu. Mary's mother had taught the language of prejudice
by using 'Pakis' in a derogatory tone. Prejudice existed on
both sides. However, racism existed on Mary's side only,
because she belonged to the majority group who held
power.

In educators, prejudice, narrowing of roles, stereotyping,
racism and its equivalent in relating to disability and
handicap all impede children's ability to inspect their own
thinking and assumptions. They put children's thinking
into narrow grooves which cut across the educational
principles explored in this book.

6 Overcoming stranger fear with positive strategies

People like to be comfortable. Thinking new thoughts, meeting new ideas, changing your ways are all inevitably uncomfortable. They involve moving out of a rut, modifying attitudes and acting differently from before. In this book, Piaget's theory of self-regulation (his equilibratory process) has often been referred to. It has two aspects. The first involves taking into yourself situations, events, experiences, which fit with what you already know, which do not require the person to modify the structures within them. The second involves meeting a situation, experience, event which does not fit with what is already known, and which requires a change in the structures within the person, and modification in his/her behaviour.

When ET met the little boy in the film of that name, he was terrified; so was the little boy. They both initially experienced stranger fear on a vast scale. Seven-year-old Elisabeth had grown up in Dorset. She had never met an African person. Her parents invited an African student to earn some holiday money by digging their garden for them. He agreed and began work. Elisabeth kept going into the garden, peeping at him and, when her friend arrived, giggling and looking at him from a distance as if he were someone from outer space. Her parents, unaware of this reaction, did not introduce her to him, which would have helped her to see him as a person. Her stranger fear persisted.

Mixing with a wide variety of people helps to break down stranger fear, provided that positive strategies are developed which support the situation. Where children do not meet in a positive atmosphere, prejudice based on ignorance and stranger fear persists and can even be exacerbated. Attitudes to disability are more likely to change if disabled people are part of the whole, rather than in institutions away from the community. This approval requires more input of resources rather than less, and unless this is understood, the chance of effective integration is slight. As Mary Warnock said in her Dimbleby lecture in 1985 of her 1978 Report on Special Educational Needs, the implementation of the recommendations made has largely been 'bungled' in the 1981 Education Act, mainly through lack of adequate resources.

At a market in Halifax, a family (two parents and two children five and eight years old) went to buy some lino.

They were talking in a relaxed manner with the man selling it. The father noticed a slit in a part being measured, and pointed it out. 'Don't worry — I'll sell that to a Paki,' said the salesman. The father and mother exchanged looks and the father said, 'We don't like that sort of talk. We hope you wouldn't sell that to anyone.' The seller replied that the father didn't know these people and that they'd trick you if they could. The father suggested that the seller was about to trick him if he hadn't pointed out the slit, and the mother told the salesman that she worked with people of Pakistani origin who were her friends and that she had never been tricked. The family did not buy the lino. The children in that family were being given a powerful role model by their parents. Racial prejudice based on ignorance and stranger fear was not to be tolerated, even if it meant unpleasantness in public.

With his parents, seven-year-old Tom was watching the TV news which was reporting on the situation in South Africa. Afterwards he said, 'If we lived there, Christopher and me wouldn't be allowed to go to school together, would we?' He was trying to sort out the implications for him and his black friend of living in an apartheid setting. He was beginning to inspect his own thinking about the structure of societies and their relevance to the world, his friends and himself.

Resources

Attitudes which promote the guiding principles discussed in this chapter are of no consequence without action. Action requires resources. Teachers need varying degrees of additional information, advice, support, special materials and amended environments if they are to work with individuals with differences. For example, integrating a visually-handicapped child will mean extra specialist teaching support in the form of peripatetic advisers qualified in the education of visually-handicapped children; additional technical equipment including braillers; microcomputers with voice output; a special materials service of braille books and tape-recorded materials; special lighting; and readiness on the part of the teacher to go for in-service training.

A teacher coming fresh to a class with minority ethnic groups should be encouraged to go on a racism awareness course; should have access to information packs and teaching materials relevant to the cultures represented in the class; should have access to at least very basic conversational language training if English is the second language; and should have teaching and support staff colleagues coming from the minority groups represented in the school.

In too many instances these resources are either not available or only available after much pressure and representation. But it is the teacher's responsiblity to press for the resources necessary to do a professional job; and it can be the responsibility of parents to use official channels and ultimately political channels (through their local elected representative) to achieve the right level of resources.

Conclusion

This chapter has used the six assertions made by Yvonne Conolly as a framework through which to explore commonalities between people, and the individuality and differences between them. A range of issues was identified as of critical importance in approaching any child's education. These included the consideration of class, race, gender and special needs.

The parts and the whole need to relate. Children need a sense of belonging, to choose their own identity and have a sense of self-worth. Everyone needs to inspect his/her own thinking and actions, confront assumptions and move towards equality of regard for all people. Fear of strangers impedes this process, and needs to be tackled directly.

Practical strategies involve knowledge of self and of others. There is a need for a broad curriculum pursued in depth which includes study going beyond the dominant culture. It should help children to link what they learn to what they already know so that a meaningful context is built around their knowledge.

Early childhood educators are in positions of power for breaking down narrow roles for children, or combating stereotyping of all kinds. The definition of racism from Katz (1978) described earlier can be slightly altered to read:

10 Evaluation and Assessment — learning from experience in working with young children

This chapter is in three parts. The first establishes what evaluation and assessment mean in the context of early childhood education. The second part looks at how teachers can gain confidence as they evaluate and assess their work. The third part relates evaluation and assessment to the early childhood principles which have been re-examined throughout this book.

What is evaluation and assessment?

It is important to distinguish between evaluation and assessment. Barry MacDonald (1982) asserts that evaluating a child's education involves examining the education that child receives. Assessment is concerned with looking at the child's progress, and his/her reactions to the education provided. Through evaluation and assessment teachers become involved in looking at both what they offer children and how this is acted upon by the children.

Wynne Harlen (1982) encourages teachers to lead the process, and sees this as a positive way to work with children and their families. She argues (Harlen, 1982, p. 190) that it is necessary 'to involve teachers in discussing the need for evaluation, analysing real problems and seeing for themselves where certain techniques are appropriate'. She asserts: 'Solutions produced by others were not seen as helpful by teachers unless the thinking which had gone into them was experienced at first hand.' This approach leads to teachers becoming more articulate about progress children

make, which is essential if parents are to have confidence in
the teacher and his/her method, and to help more in the
learning process. For example, in the Oxford studies (Sylva
et al., 1980), after teachers listened to tape recordings of·
their conversations in the classroom they subsequently increased the quality of their interactions with children. With
modern tape recorders, self-taping is now very easy.

Evaluation and assessment require teachers to be clear
about their intentions, and how they will act upon them.
This means knowing about child development and the early
childhood curriculum, and keeping up to date with recent
research and thinking. New in-service training is an essential aspect of this approach to evaluation and assessment.

Formative and summative methods of evaluation and
assessment

If 'the best' is seen as only that which is measurable, that
part of education which is offered to young children
becomes narrower and narrower.

Formative methods are those where the process of evaluation and assessment is continual — say, regularly collecting
paintings or photographing models. This contrasts with
summative record-keeping which takes a snapshot at the
same point in time and compares the results to national
norms. For example, twice a year children might be given a
reading test; or the Keele Record cards (Tyler, 1978) might
be filled in by the teacher for every child at a certain point in
the nursery school year.

Both kinds of record keeping are necessary, for they give
important information and clues about the kind of education the child is receiving and his/her development. Summative methods show where children stand in relation to
national norms, and norms within that particular group of
children. They focus on what can be measured. Formative
methods keep a balance, as Denny Taylor (1983) says,
'acting and reacting', and also emphasising how children
are developing over a period, in everyday contexts rather
than test situations. The latter are important because
children perform at a higher level in meaningful contexts
than they do in formal test situations, where they cannot
easily assess what is required of them by adults (Hughes,
1983). All teachers use formative methods to a greater or
lesser extent. What is argued here is that these should be

more formalised and made more explicit so that parents can recognise them.

Using both formative and summative methods of evaluation and assessment education in early childhood supports the interactionist approach to early childhood education. Using one or the other does not and has severe disadvantages. For example, one of the problems of summative methods is that what is measured quickly becomes what children ought to know. Children become 'moulded' to fit the test. Wohwill (1970; quoted in Almy, 1975, p. 53) highlights this problem.

> While narrowly defined, stepwise organised learning sequences may result in limited success with respect to the specific content area at which the learning material is directed, the young child is not apt to make the generalisations to other related concepts or concepts of his own. However, he is apt to achieve concepts perhaps more slowly, but on a broader front, if presented with a more loosely structured, at the same time more wide-ranging, experiential context, such as would allow the imagination freer range.

Using only summative methods of record-keeping ignores the interactive approach to early childhood education. Focusing too much on narrow, measurable progress contradicts the early childhood principles.

On the other hand, only using formative methods of record-keeping focuses too much upon processes and ignores the product. While it is essential for teachers to emphasise their own development as a contribution to the child's development, part of the communication of the process must lie in being able to show some results. Understanding the reading process is central — but showing what children can read also matters! The Thomas Report (ILEA, 1984) points out that there needs to be a sensible balance between the experiences children have and activities they are involved in, and their output — the evidence in terms of records of the work done.

Evaluation and assessment are important to parents. For example, at school Open Evenings they often seize upon written work, drawings, paintings, models, or sum books. They want to see what their child has done — and to compare this with what other children do. Parents enjoy 'performances' of music, drama and dance, because again there is a product to see. These are often the only available means they have of putting their child's achievements, or their anxieties about their child's progress, into any kind of context. The anxieties parents experience about their child's progress cannot be stressed too strongly.

A painting is often seized on by parents because it gives a tangible product to see.

The advantage of using explicit formative as well as summative approaches is that parents, and others such as school governors, are included in the process of education. They are helped to examine the education offered to the child beyond the superficial level, which tends to be entrenched in the education they themselves received. They can be supported in doing so by teachers who are confident and articulate, who constantly seek to improve the service, and are flexible in their thinking which is based on sound conceptually-based knowledge.

They can be helped to see a broad and more wide-ranging picture of the child develop over a period of time, based on the continual observations made, and on the plans formulated in the curriculum. Their involvement in this process, working with the teacher, illuminates the process in the way that Wynne Harlen suggests brings results. Parents are then in a position to take pleasure in their child's strengths, and to tackle the weaker areas supported by the school. Seeing an individual 'interest book' develop as part of class work, or seeing different paintings displayed on the classroom wall and then made into another kind of interest book, are examples of this way of working. Parents are also able to see their child's progress in relation to other children in a less unpalatable way than when suddenly plunged into an Open Evening, where the differences between their child's achievement and the achievements of others may be startling.

Gaining confidence through evaluation and assessment

Confident teachers have two strengths. The first is the ability to reflect upon, analyse and act upon their work with children. This will take place within the setting of a conceptually cohesive understanding of child development, a grasp of different areas of knowledge and an appreciation of how to put the two together.

The second strength of confident teachers is the ability to communicate these strengths to colleagues, the child's family and those beyond the school setting, to explain effectively what they are doing and gain external co-operation. In particular, teachers need continually to broaden their knowledge of how children develop. They need to be able to observe children with skill, and use their observations in practice. Alongside this, teachers need to develop their understanding of different and wide areas of knowledge, and to see logical lines of development in them (Harlen, 1982). In each case they need to be able to discuss observations and action plans with colleagues, the child's family, and beyond the school setting.

Developing these two strengths requires time and effort in planning and reflecting on work with children, colleagues and the child's family. Teachers who have a clear approach are less likely to jump on to the latest educational bandwaggon. Because they are striving to put recent developments into some coherent framework within which to set their practice, they are less likely to get in a rut, and more able to establish where they need to modify or change their practice.

Half-formed ideas are easily challenged, and this quickly threatens self-confidence. Teachers who are helped to think about what they do (through staff meetings, in-service training and so on), are in a position to justify their actions. This means that they can share their thinking. They can meet differing ideas about education from a firm base, and do so with self-confidence.

It is one thing to be able to look at other points of view, but it is also necessary to examine these in relation to one's own. Not having a point of view, or not knowing quite what one's point of view is, does not enhance self-esteem. Those with low self-esteem are often held in low esteem by others.

Communication begins within the profession — through initial and in-service training, and by developing whole school policies through staff discussions and working together. Communication is shared with the child's family, through open-style record-keeping which invites partnership. It goes beyond this to others within the profession. Efforts should be made to improve communication between early childhood educators and secondary level educators, for example. There is also a need for multi-professional work, with co-operation, co-ordination and sharing as the key.

The general public needs to be better informed. The confident, articulate conceptually-knowledgeable teacher can invite discussion. If people understand the work being done, they are more likely to value it.

Relating evaluation and assessment to the early childhood principles

Having a clear framework for working with children means having principles which are borne in mind, as a backcloth against which work is set. Indeed, evaluation and assessment can only be applied if they are co-ordinated with aims. Put simply, it is not sensible to check how well one is progressing unless one has a destination — or at least a direction — in mind.

This section gives a broad framework of evaluation and assessment appropriate to early childhood education, through looking at the ten principles outlined in chapter 2.

1 Childhood is a part of life as well as a preparation for the future

In terms of evaluation and assessment, this means that what is offered must be relevant for future knowledge as well as appropriate for the moment.

2 The whole child is considered to be important

Records need to be kept of all aspects of the child's development. There are multi-professional implications in this. Health records are confidential, but it is of central importance for those professionals responsible for the child's health to work with those responsible for the child's education, since the two aspects inevitably link. It is also important to bear in mind the child's strengths and weaknesses. This becomes of even more importance when assessing a child with any kind of special need. Specialists of all kinds (medical, social workers, educational psychologists and educators) may need to share and build vital information together with the parent. Building records together can enable early diagnosis or monitoring of special needs, temporary or permanent. This approach is particularly helpful in the field of health surveillance, and as a means of offering appropriate help in terms of preventive treatment, remediation, or dealing with handicap.

3   Learning and knowledge cannot be compartmentalised:
    everything links

Emphasising a broad, integrated curriculum reasserts this
principle, and provides a yardstick for teacher-led evaluation and assessment of the adequacy of the curriculum. A
broad context enables children to practise newly emerging
thinking in a variety of settings. The child who is an
emergent reader of print might also be one of musical notation. The child who is beginning to tell stories, which the
teacher writes down, can also choreograph a dance which
the teacher helps to shape, or compose music which the
teacher writes down.

4 and 5   Intrinsic motivation and child-initiated,
          self-directed activity is valued; self-discipline is
          emphasised

Assessing whether children are able to initiate, or whether
they depend on others to goad them into action, requires
close observation and recording what they choose to do,
what spontaneous or planned work excites and catches their
interest. These will give the adult clues about what is likely
to encourage the child's intrinsic motivation to flourish.
Recent empirical research (e.g. Wells and Nicholls, 1985;
Donaldson *et al.*, 1983) emphasises the need to 'use' the
child's initiatives and intrinsic motivation, rather than cut
across these. As part of this, the adult needs to see if conversations, activities and group times are promoting the child's
initiatives and motivations, or dominating and damaging
them.
   The teacher needs to observe and occasionally record how
often he/she imposes control and discipline on the child;
and to what extent children have self-discipline and can
curb themselves. This is particularly important where a
child has behavioural problems. Recognising and praising
increases in self-discipline, and noting progress, fosters
feelings of self-worth.

6   There are specially receptive periods of learning at
    different stages of development

The more the adult can establish the exact stage of development of the child, the better. Check-lists on norms of

development (e.g. Sheridan, 1973) can be helpful. Looking at key areas of development can help, as in Principle 2, the importance of the whole child. The Piagetian schema is a useful mechanism for giving detail in this.

It is necessary to use a child's intrinsic motivation, rather than cut across it.

Record-keeping which attempts to identify the schema, to plot its level, and to see how the child uses the environment and responds to teacher initiatives in relation to it, helps to fill in some of the details. It is not possible to rescue someone lost in a wood if you do not know where they are.

7 What children can do should be the starting point in a child's education

This kind of assessment requires summative procedures. It relates to Vygotsky's (1978) zone of actual development and shows what children can do unaided (e.g. use scissors). However, this will only indicate one half of development. The other half of what children can do is to be found in the shared activities supported by adults. This requires formative assessment — intuitions continually interpreted as they are analysed and articulated. The result is interest books and classroom displays which show the children's achievement, what they can do, in a different context from the unaided 'test'. Empirical evidence widely supports Principle 7, typified by Turiel and Weston (1983) who looked at children's understanding of rules with moral implications.

Lawrence K. Franks' view (quoted in Almy, 1975, p. 222) supports assessment of what a child can do.

> Some people learn and have a preference for visual experiences and later for reading, and then there are those who prefer and learn through tactile and haptic contacts.

8 There is an inner life in the child which emerges under favourable conditions

Recording is central to assessing the emerging symbolic processes. Providing for emerging symbolic functioning and fostering it during the early years require skill and planning. A well-provisioned classroom will not do this on its own. Record-keeping needs to take account of how provision is used by children. This might lead to noting conversations, requests, questions, or annotation in relation to paintings, drawings, models, dances and songs made by the children. The children's products show only the tip of the iceberg. Records must reveal the iceberg itself. As Wynne Harlen (1982) points out, this takes time and effort. Taking photographs, making individual interest books, using the child's drawings, can provide a useful record which can be shared with the family and others if appropriate. It encourages children to reflect on work they have done over a period of time as well as recently, and gives a long-term picture of what the child has been learning. Record-keeping of this kind is an integral part of classroom practice, and becomes a shared and worthwhile pleasure rather than a chore. As Wynne Harlen (1982) asserts, teachers gain who lead positively on evaluation and assessment — and so do the children and their families.

9 The people (both adults and children) with whom the child interacts are of central importance

Assessment of children's development is only possible if work displayed on walls and in books is their own. A parent at an Open Day said to Harry (aged three), 'What a lovely train. You clever boy to do that.' It was a template outline of a steam train, which had prints from cotton reels on it. Harry said, 'I only did those' (meaning the cotton reel prints). The teacher had had the idea of making a train to fit a project on transport. She cut out the template and demanded that Harry print on it. All this illustrates is that he can follow a simple instruction — and print on an outline — a very low-level achievement unworthy of the label 'creative'. Teacher-dominated displays, although attractive, reveal a very low level of achievement which underestimate what children can do.

In contrast, displays of work initiated and carried through by children, given adult support, demonstrate what *children* can do. The children's work can be beautifully mounted by adults and, where appropriate, explanatory notes about the contents or process of the work (since the result may not be obvious; e.g. a blob of paint on a page is representing a ball bouncing) can be given. This method shows the adult's role as supporting, extending, what the child can do (Vygotsky's zone of potential development), then sharing this through the classroom display, which illuminates the child's work but does not take it over.

10 The child's education is seen as an interaction between the child and the environment, including other people and knowledge itself

In chapter 4 it was suggested that the early childhood curriculum involves a process with three aspects:

(a) the child;
(b) the areas of knowledge to be taught;
(c) the environment in which this takes place (people, places, objects and events).

This leads to evaluation of the way in which (b) and (c) are introduced, and assessment of the child, (a), in relation to them. There will, as a result of these different emphases, need to be a variety of forms of record-keeping.

For example, a flow chart may be useful in highlighting all three aspects, both in the long- and short-term planning which is necessary. Flow charts allow (b) and (c) to develop in synchrony, and safeguard balance and breadth as well as depth of curriculum. They allow for flexibility in the order in which knowledge is introduced and the possibility of constantly adding to the chart. Some aspects can be left out if they become inappropriate or irrelevant as the work develops. In this way general plans and possibilities, carefully thought out, can emerge, but individuals can be catered for. Flow charts can be shared with parents. Some teachers pin them on the walls for parents to see.

There is a tendency to become immersed in the evaluation aspect and to ignore the assessment aspect. If flow charts are to be of use, there is a constant need to relate the child and the chart. The developing plan should become a formative assessment of the child, and a formative evaluation of what is offered. For example, the child's name may be added to the flow chart, and dated, to show when he or she became involved in an aspect of the chart. This can be cross-referenced to the child's individual record, where more detail can be given. Other forms of record-keeping will emphasise assessment only.

Check-lists (can jump, use scissors, and so on) and Keele records, for example, indicate progression in some aspects of development. There is a paucity of record-keeping methods which help teachers to assess development in certain areas of the curriculum — for example, movement, music, art, religious education and science. Unless these areas are dealt with, it is difficult to evaluate what is offered, since development and curriculum are synchronised if the interactionist approach is maintained. If record-keeping is to contribute to classroom practice teachers need to think carefully about which forms of record-keeping are most helpful. Audrey Curtis (1986,

p. 137) points out that teachers need to be clear about what they wish to record.

Summary

Each early childhood principle has a contemporary implication for evaluation and assessment

In the area of evaluation

(a)   There is a need to draw up lines of development in each area of knowledge, beginning with what the child can manage.

(b)   The breadth of the curriculum must be given attention in record-keeping.

(c)   Records which are an integrated part of classroom practice are not onerous, and are very useful.

(d)   Classroom display should be seen as a form of record-keeping, rather than an opportunity for teachers to demonstrate their own artistic abilities with children's work as the vehicle for this.

In the area of assessment

(a)   Multi-professional approaches to record-keeping require attention. In the case of children with special needs, they are essential. They need to highlight strengths and weaknesses in the child.

(b)   Record-keeping needs to show the processes whereby children have initiated or shown what motivates them to operate at the highest level of which they are capable. Records and displays which are integrated into classroom practice promote this.

(c)   Record-keeping needs to give sufficient detail of the child's stage of development to help the teacher make appropriate provision.

(d)   Record-keeping needs to demonstrate what children can achieve unaided as well as what they can achieve when supported. It should concentrate on strengths first, since through these weaknesses can be tackled.

(e)   The way links are made from the child to the areas of knowledge needs to be recorded continually, through noting the way provision is manipulated.

Conclusion

Teachers need to feel strong in the work to which they are
committed. They are then in a position to develop and communicate their work. They need to see evaluation and
assessment as useful instruments illuminating and highlighting the value of what they strive to do, and useful
indicators of areas which need attention and rethinking. In
this way, they can identify for themselves their strengths
and weaknesses.

11 The Way Forward

The aim of this book has not been to prescribe how adults should work with young children. Rather it has been to provide a framework within which to work with some confidence that the approach will be consistent and be based on established theory and recent research. Detailed methods of work must depend on the individual adult and, most importantly, on the child him/herself, and the family and socio-cultural setting.

The basis of the framework is the 10 principles of early childhood education which are once again set out below (number 8 has been slightly reworded to make the language more contemporary). They are:

1 Childhood is seen as valid in itself, as a part of life and not simply as preparation for adulthood. Thus education is seen similarly as something of the present and not just preparation and training for later.

2 The whole child is considered to be important. Health, physical and mental, is emphasised, as well as the importance of feelings and thinking and spiritual aspects.

3 Learning is not compartmentalised, for everything links.

4 Intrinsic motivation, resulting in child-initiated, self-directed activity, is valued.

5 Self-discipline is emphasised.

6 There are specially receptive periods of learning at different stages of development.

7 What children can do (rather than what they cannot do) is the starting point in the child's education.

8 There is an inner structure in the child which includes the imagination and which emerges especially under favourable conditions.

9 The people (both adults and children) with whom the child interacts are of central importance.

10 The child's education is seen as an interaction between the child and the environment the child is in — including, in particular, other people and knowledge itself.

From these principles, and taking account of prevailing practice as well as policy pressures, the following action points are proposed.

I   There needs to be more emphasis on partnership and reciprocity between adults and children. This requires better understanding of child development and of the different areas of knowledge.

II   While recognising the importance of being child-centred, there is a need to become more family-centred.

III There is a need for better and more multi-professional exchanges between workers and services, including voluntary agencies.

IV   It is essential to have a better conceptual articulation of what good early childhood education is, with appropriate assessment and evaluation which does not cut across its valuable traditions.

The past leads to the future through the present. Heraclitis said:

You can put your hand in the river once.
You cannot put your hand in the same river twice.

References and Bibliography

ALMY, M. (1975) *The Early Childhood Educator at Work*. New York: McGraw-Hill.

ANDERSON, A. and STOKES, S. (1984) 'Social and institutional influences on the development and practice of literacy', in SMITH, F., GOELMAN, H. and OBERG, A. (eds) *Awakening to Literacy*. London: Heinemann.

ATHEY, C. (1972–7) Report of the Leverhulme/Gulbenkian Froebel Research Project.

ATHEY, C. (1980) 'Parental involvement in nursery education'. *Early Childhood*, 1, 3, December.

ATHEY, C. (1981) 'Parental involvement in nursery education'. *Early Child Development and Care*, 7, 4, 253–67.

BARTHOLOMEW, L. (1985) 'It's all very well in theory, but what about in practice?' *Early Child Development and Care*, 19, 3, 237–51.

BENNETT, N. and DESFORGES, C. (1984) *The Quality of Pupil Learning Experiences*. Hillsdale, NJ: Erlbaum.

BERRUETA-CLEMENT, J. R., SCHWEINHART, L. J., BARNETT, W. S., EPSTEIN, A. and WEIKART, D. P. (1984) *Changed Lives: The effects of the Perry Pre-school Program on youth through age 19 years*. Monograph of the High Scope Educational Research Foundation no. 8. Ypsilanti, MI: High Scope Press.

BOWER, T. (1974) *Development in Infancy*. Oxford: Freeman.

BOWLBY, J. (1958) *Can I Leave my Baby?* London: National Association for Mental Health.

BRENNAN, M. (1978) BBC TV 'Horizon' programme: Talking Hands.

BRICE HEATH, S. (1983) *Ways with Words*. Cambridge: Cambridge University Press.

BRUCE, T. (1976) 'A comparative study of the Montessori Method, and a Piaget-based conceptualisation of the pre-school curriculum'. Unpublished MA dissertation, University of London.

BRUCE, T. (1978) 'Side by side. Montessori and other educational principles'. Montessori Society AMI (UK) Third Annual Weekend Conference, February.

BRUCE, T. (1984) 'A Froebelian looks at Montessori's work'. *Early Child Development and Care*, 14, Vols 1 and 2.

BRUCE, T. (1985) 'It's all very well in practice, but what about in theory?' *Early Child Development and Care*, 19, 3, 151–73.

BRUNER, J. (1960; 1977) *The Process of Education.* Cambridge, MA: Harvard University Press.

BRUNER, J. (1968) *Toward a Theory of Instruction.* Cambridge, MA: Harvard University Press.

BRUNER, J. (1972) *The Relevance of Education.* London: Allen and Unwin.

BRUNER, J. (1974) *Beyond the Information Given.* London: Allen and Unwin.

BRUNER, J. (1980) *Under Five in Britain: The Oxford Pre-school Research Project.* Oxford: Grant McIntyre (Blackwell).

BRUNER, J. (1981) 'What is representation?', in ROBERTS, M. and TAMBURRINI, J. (eds) *Child Development 0-5.* Edinburgh: Holmes McDougall.

BRUNER, J., WOOD, D. and ROSS, G. (1976) 'The role of tutoring in problem-solving'. *Journal of Child Psychology and Psychiatry,* 17, 89-100.

BUTLER, D. (1980) *Babies Need Books.* London: Bodley Head.

CALKINS, LUCY McCORMICK (1983) *Lessons from a Child, on the teaching and learning of writing.* London: Heinemann.

CHUKOVSKY, K. (1963) *From Two to Five.* Berkeley, CA: University of California Press.

CLAY, M. (1975) *What did I Write?* London: Heinemann.

CLIFT. P., CLEAVE, S. and GRIFFIN, M. (1980) *The Aims, Role and Deployment of Staff in the Nursery.* Windsor: NFER.

CONOLLY, Y. (1983) Organisation Mondiale pour l'Education Prescolaire (OMEP; World Organisation for Early Childhood Education) Conference, London.

CORSARO, W. (1979) '"We're friends, right?" Children's use of access rituals in a nursery school'. *Language in Society,* 8, 315-36.

CURTIS, A. (1986) *A Curriculum for the Pre-school Child.* Windsor: NFER-Nelson.

DAVIES, M. (1969) 'Movement', in BREARLEY, M. (ed.) *Fundamentals in the First School.* Oxford: Blackwell.

DAVIES, M. (1977) *Movement and Young Children.* Unpublished Curriculum Paper, Froebel College, Roehampton Institute of Higher Education, London.

DEARDEN, R. F. (1968) *The Philosophy of Primary Education* London: Routledge and Kegan Paul.

DEPARTMENT OF EDUCATION AND SCIENCE (1975) *A Language for Life* (The Bullock Report). London: HMSO.

DEPARTMENT OF EDUCATION AND SCIENCE (1978) *Special Educational Needs: Report of the Committee of Enquiry into the Education of Handicapped Children and Young People* (The Warnock Report). London: HMSO.

DOMBEY, H. (1983) 'Learning the language of books', in Meek, M. (ed.) *Opening Moves.* Bedford Way Papers no. 17, University of London Institute of Education.

DONALDSON, M. (1978) *Children's Minds*. London: Collins/Fontana.

DONALDSON, M., GRIEVE, R. and PRATT, C. (eds) (1983) *Early Childhood Development and Education*. Oxford: Blackwell.

DOUGLAS, J. W. B. (1964) *The Home and the School*. London: MacGibbon and Kee.

DUNN, J. (1984) *Sisters and Brothers*. London: Collins/Fontana.

EDMUND, F. (1979) *Rudolf Steiner Education. The Waldorf Schools*. London: Rudolf Steiner Press.

ELLIOTT, M. (1985) *Preventing Child Sexual Assault*. London: Bedford Square Press.

ENGELMANN, S. (1971) 'Does the Piagetian approach imply instruction?', in ROSS GREEN, D., FORD, M. and FLAMER, G. (eds) *Measurement and Piaget*. New York: McGraw-Hill.

ERIKSON, E. (1963) *Childhood and Society*. London: Routledge and Kegan Paul.

FERREIRO, E. and TEBEROSKY, A. (1983) *Literacy before Schooling* (trans. Karen Goodman Castro). London: Heinemann.

FOX, C. (1983) 'Talking like a book', in MEEK, M. (ed.) *Opening Moves*. Bedford Way Papers no. 17, University of London Institute of Education.

FROEBEL, F. W. (1878) *Mother Play and Nursery Songs* (trans. Fanny E. Dwight [songs] and Josephine Jarvis [prose]). Boston, MA: Lee and Shepard.

FROEBEL, F. W. (1887) *The Education of Man* New York: Appleton.

GARDNER, H. (1982) *Developmental Psychology*. Boston, MA: Little, Brown.

GARRARD, H. (1986) Personal communication.

GARVEY, C. (1977) *Play*. The Developing Child series; BRUNER, J., COLE, M. and LLOYD, B. (eds). London: Collins/Fontana–Open Books.

GESELL, A. (1954) *The First Five Years of Life*. London: Methuen.

GINSBURG, H. and OPPER, S. (1979) *Piaget's Theory of Intellectual Development*. Englewood Cliffs, NJ: Prentice-Hall.

GOODMAN, KENNETH and YETTA (1977) 'Miscue analysis'. *Harvard Educational Review*, 47, 3.

GOODMAN, Y. (1980) 'The roots of literacy'. Paper presented at the annual meeting of the Claremont Reading Conference, January.

GOODMAN, Y. (1984) 'The development of initial literacy', in SMITH, F., GOELMAN, H. and OBERG, A. (eds) *Awakening to Literacy*. London: Heinemann.

GOODNOW, J. (1977) *Children's Drawings*. The Developing Child series: BRUNER, J. COLE, M. and LLOYD, B. (eds). London: Collins/Fontana–Open Books.

GRAVES, D. (1983) *Writing: Teachers and children at work*. London: Heinemann.

GREGORY, R. (1982) *Assembly Line: A tape-slide programme.* Bedfordshire Education Service.

GRIFFIN, P. (1986) Article in *The Times Educational Supplement,* 15 August.

HALSEY, A. H. (ed.) (1972) *Educational Priority: Report of a research project sponsored by the DES and SSRC. Vol. 1 EPA Problems and Policies.* London: HMSO.

HARLEN, W. (1982) 'Evaluation and assessment', in RICHARDS, C. (ed.) *New Directions in Primary Education.* London: Falmer Press.

HOLDAWAY, D. (1979) *The Foundations of Literacy.* Gosford, NSW, Australia: Ashton Scholastic.

HONIG, A. (1984) 'Working in partnership with parents of handicapped infants'. *Early Child Development and Care,* 14, 1-2, 13-36.

HUGHES, M. *et al.* (1980) *Nurseries Now.* Harmondsworth: Penguin Books.

HUGHES, M. (1983) 'What's difficult about learning arithmetic?', in DONALDSON, M., GRIEVE, R. and PRATT, C. (eds) *Childhood Development and Education.* Oxford: Blackwell.

HUGHES, M. (1986) *Children and Number: Difficulties in Learning Mathematics.* Oxford: Blackwell.

INNER LONDON EDUCATION AUTHORITY (ILEA) (1985) *Improving Primary Schools.* A Report by Norman Thomas. London: ILEA.

ISAACS, S. (1968) *The Nursery Years.* London: Routledge and Kegan Paul.

JACKSON, B. (1979) *Starting School.* London: Croom Helm.

KAMII, C. and DEVRIES, R. (1977) 'Piaget for early years', in DAY, M. and PARKER, R. (eds) *The Pre-school in Action: Exploring Early Childhood Programs* (2nd edition). Newton, MA: Allyn and Bacon.

KAPLAN, L. (1978) *Oneness and Separateness: From infant to individual.* New York: Simon and Schuster. Quoted in HONIG, A.

KELLMER PRINGLE, M. (1974; 1980, 2nd edition) *The Needs of Children.* London: Hutchinson.

KILPATRICK, W. (1915) *Montessori Examined.* London: Constable and Co.

LANE, HARLEN (1977) *The Wild Boy of Aveyron.* London: Allen and Unwin.

LEAT, D. (1977) *Towards a Definition of Volunteer Involvement.* Berkhamsted: The Volunteer Centre.

LIEBSCHNER, J. (1985) 'Children learning through each other'. *The Link,* Froebel Institute, London; also *Early Child Development and care,* 21, 1-3, 121-35.

MACDONALD, B. (1982) 'Evaluation and assessment', in RICHARDS, C. (ed.) *New Directions in Primary Education.* London: Falmer Press.

MCGEENEY, P. (1980) 'The involvement of parents', in CRAFT, M. et al. (eds) *Linking Home and School* (3rd edition). London: Harper and Row.

MCKELLER, P. (1957) *Imagination and Thinking*. London: Cohen and West.

MCLAUGHLIN, B. (1980) *Second Language Acquisition in Childhood*. Hillsdale, NJ: Erlbaum.

MATTHEW, C. and J. (1983) *Early Mathematics Experiences*. Reading, MA: Addison-Wesley.

MATTHEWS, J. (1983) 'Children drawing: are young children really scribbling?' Paper presented to British Psychological Society, Cardiff.; also (1984) *Early Child Development and Care*, 18, 1-2, 1-41.

MEEK, M. (1985) 'Play and paradoxes: Some considerations of imagination and language', in WELLS, G. and NICHOLLS, J. (eds) *Language and Learning: An Interactional Perspective*. London: Falmer Press.

MILNE, A. A. (1926) *Winnie the Pooh*. London: Methuen.

MONTESSORI, M. (1912) *The Montessori Method*. London: Heinemann.

MONTESSORI, M. (1949) *The Absorbent Mind*. Adyar, Madras, India: Theosophical Publishing House.

MONTESSORI, M. (1975) *The Child in the Family* (trans. Nancy Rockmore Cirillo). London: Pan.

NEWSON, E. (1972) 'Towards an understanding of the parental role', in *The Parental Role* (Papers from annual conference). London: National Children's Bureau.

NICHOLLS, R. (ed.), with SEDGEWICK, J., DUNCAN, J., CURWEN, L. and MCDOUGALL, B. (1986) *Rumpus Schema Extra*. Cleveland Teachers in Education (LEA).

NUFFIELD MATHEMATICS PROJECT (1967) *I Do and I Understand. Beginnings*. Edinburgh: Chambers; London: Murray.

PIAGET, J. (1962) *Play, Dreams and Imitation in Childhood*. London: Routledge and Kegan Paul.

PIAGET, J. (1968) *Six Psychological Studies*. London: University of London Press Ltd.

PIAGET, J. and INHELDER, B. (1969) *The Psychology of the Child*. London: Routledge and Kegan Paul.

POLANYI, M. (1958) *Personal Knowledge*. London: Routledge and Kegan Paul.

POULTON, L. and G. (1979) 'Neighbourhood support for young families'. *Early Child Development and Care*, 6, 1-2, 73-83.

PROVENZO, E. and BRETT, A. (1983) *The Complete Block Book*. Syracuse, NY: Syracuse University Press.

PUGH, G. and De'ATH, E. (1984) *The Needs of Parents*. London: Macmillan.

ROBERTS, M. and TAMBURRINI, J. (eds) (1981) *Child Development 0-5*. Edinburgh: Holmes McDougall.

ROBERTS, S. (1977) *Early Learning in Mathematics.* Unpublished Curriculum Paper, Froebel College, Roehampton Institute of Higher Education, London.

ROSS GREEN, D., FORD, M. and FLAMER, G. (eds) (1971) *Measurement and Piaget.* New York: McGraw-Hill.

ROUSSEAU, J. J. (1762; 1963) *Emile* (trans. Barbara Foxley). London: Dent.

RUBIN, Z. (1983) 'The skills of friendship', in DONALDSON, M., GRIEVE, R. and PRATT, C. (eds) *Early Childhood Development and Education.* Oxford: Blackwell.

SCHEFFLER, I. (1967) 'Philosophical models of teaching', in PETERS, R. S. (ed.) *The Concept of Education.* London: Routledge and Kegan Paul.

SHARP, A. (1986) *The Learning and Development of Three- to Five-year-olds. Schema.* City of Sheffield Education Department.

SHERIDAN, M. (1973) *Children's Developmental Progress from Birth to Five Years.* Windsor: NFER.

SMILANSKY, S. (1968) *The Effects of Socio-dramatic Play on Disadvantaged Preschool Children.* New York: John Wiley.

SMITH, F. (1983) *Essays into Literacy.* London: Heinemann

STEEDMAN, C. (1982) *The Tidy House.* London: Virago.

STEEDMAN, C. (1986) 'The mother made conscious. The historical development of a primary school pedagogy'. *History Workshop Journal,* 20.

STEINER, RUDOLF (1926) *The Essentials of Education.* London: Anthroposophical Publishing Co.

STEINER, RUDOLF (1965) *The Education of the Child.* London: Rudolf Steiner Press.

STONE, M. (1981) *The Education of the Black Child in Britain.* London: Collins/ Fontana.

STRAUSS, M. (1978) *Understanding Children's Drawings.* London: Rudolf Steiner Press.

SYLVA, K., ROY, C. and PAINTER, M. (1980) *Childwatching at Playgroup and Nursery School (Oxford Pre-school Research Project).* Oxford: Grant McIntyre (Blackwell).

SYLVA, K., SMITH, T. and MOORE, E. (1986) *Monitoring the High Scope Training Program, 1984–5. Final Report.* Department of Social and Administrative Studies, University of Oxford.

TAMBURRINI, J. (1982) 'New directions in nursery education', in RICHARDS, C. *New Directions in Primary Education.* London: Falmer Press.

TAYLOR, D. (1983) *Family Literacy.* London: Heinemann.

TIZARD, B. and HUGHES, M. (1984) *Young Children Learning.* London: Collins/Fontana.

TIZARD, B., MORTIMORE, J. and BURCHELL, B. (1981) *Involving Parents in Nursery and Infant Schools.* Oxford: Grant McIntyre (Blackwell).

TURIEL, E. and WESTON, D. (1983) 'Act-rule relation: Children's concepts of social rules', in DONALDSON, M., GRIEVE, R. and PRATT, C. (eds) *Early Childhood Development and Care.* Oxford: Blackwell.

TYLER, S. (1978) *Keele Pre-school Assessment Guide.* Keele University.

VYGOTSKY, L. (1978) *Mind in Society.* Cambridge, MA: Harvard University Press.

VYGOTSKY, L. (1983) 'School instruction and mental development', in DONALDSON, M., GRIEVE, R. and PRATT, C. (eds) *Early Childhood Development and Education.* Oxford: Blackwell.

WATERLAND, L. (1985) *Read with Me. An Apprenticeship Approach to Reading.* South Woodchester, Stroud: Thimble Press.

WARNOCK, M. (1985) 'Teacher Teach Thyself' (The Dimbleby Lecture). *The Listener,* 28 March.

WEBB, T. (1974) *Purpose and Practice in Nursery Education.* Oxford: Blackwell.

WELLS, G. (1981) *Learning through Interaction.* Cambridge: Cambridge University Press.

WELLS, G. (1983) 'Talking with children: the complementary roles of parents and teachers', in DONALDSON, M., GRIEVE, R. and PRATT, C. (eds) *Early Childhood Development and Education.* Oxford: Blackwell.

WELLS, G. and NICHOLLS, J. (eds) (1985) *Language and Learning: An Interactional Perspective.* London: Falmer Press.

WILES, S. (1981) 'Language issues in the multicultural classroom,' in Mercer, N. (ed.) *Language in School and Community.* London: Edward Arnold.

WILKINSON, R. (1980) *Questions and Answers on Rudolf Steiner Education.* East Grinstead: Henry Goulden.

WILLIAMS, E. and SHUARD, H. (1976) *Primary Mathematics Today.* Harlow: Longman.

WINNICOTT, D. W. (1971) *Playing and Reality.* London: Tavistock Publications; also (1974) Harmondsworth: Penguin Books.

WOHWILL, J. (1970) 'The place of structured experience in early cognitive development'. *Interchange,* 1, 2, 25.

Index